What's the
Big
Deal?
about
my
parents

Cover photo by Tony Stone Images/Ron Krisel
Cover and inside design by Ahaa! Design/Dina Sorn
Edited by Dale Reeves and Leslie Durden

Library of Congress Cataloging-in-Publication Data:
Burgen, Jim, 1962-
    What's the big deal : about my parents / Jim Burgen.
      p. cm.
    ISBN 0-7847-1252-2
    1. Christian teenagers--Religious life. 2. Parent and teenager--Religious
aspects--Christianity. [1. Parent and teenager. 2. Christian life. 3. Teenagers.
4. Adolescence.] I. Title: What's the big deal about my parents?. II. Title.
BV4531.3 .B87 2001
248.8'3--dc21

                                          2001020865

Standard Publishing, Cincinnati, Ohio.
A division of Standex International Corporation.

08   07   06   05   04   03   02

7   6   5   4   3

What's the
Big
Deal?
about
my
parents

Jim Burgen

EMPOWERED® Youth Products
Standard Publishing
Cincinnati, Ohio

contents

Chapter one
Hard, Scary Lessons 9

Chapter two
The Brady Bunch, the Partridge
Family, Joseph and Moses 21

Chapter three
Rules and Regulations 37

Chapter four
Why Obey? 49

Chapter five
How to Light Your House 61

Chapter six
The Trust Factor 79

Chapter seven
Trust . . . How Do I Get It? 89

Chapter eight
Working Out Problems 103

Chapter nine
Keep Talking and Keep Trying 117

Chapter ten
Under Attack 133

Chapter eleven
Final Thoughts 143

Bonus excerpt
from "What's the Big Deal? About Sex" 151

one

1

Hard, Scary Lessons

Chapter One

OK, I was sitting on my couch the other night. Everyone in the family was in bed. So I turned on the TV to my favorite channel, Animal Planet. (I have to confess, it's the only reason I have cable. I'm an Animal Planet junkie.) As luck would have it, my timing was perfect. My favorite nature show was on, "Wild Rescue." The show is awesome. On each episode, park rangers travel around the world rescuing wild animals in dangerous situations (thus, the name . . . duh!). On this particular episode, there were three rescues.

The first wild animal in danger was a black bear. Apparently, this bear had determined that he no longer wanted to live in the forest with the other bears so he decided to move into town. Each night, he would walk around the neighborhoods turning over garbage cans, terrorizing family pets and generally scaring the padoodle out of people (I made up that word, but you get the picture).

Well, being smart guys, the park rangers recognized this as a potentially dangerous situation to the bear, not to mention little Susie out walking her poodle on a warm summer night. They came up with a plan. The rangers set up this big barrel with a remote control trapdoor, placed some bait inside, hid in the bushes and waited. Before long, the bear showed up, went inside, the door slammed shut, they loaded the barrel onto a truck and then drove out into the mountains. The next morning they opened the door and the bear ran into the woods and lived happily ever after. I was especially touched when the park ranger with a tear in her eye confessed, "Saying good-bye is always the hard part."

The next animal to be rescued was a huge moose.

OK, at this point, you are probably thinking, "Hey, I bought a book about parents and this dude is rambling on and on about a bear and a moose." Lighten up. I'm making a point. You'll understand in a few pages. I'm creating a mood.

Anyway, this huge moose had wandered right into the business district of this town. At one point, the moose knocked this guy over and jumped up and down on him. When you weigh 1500 pounds, that's going to do some damage. So the park rangers decided, "We need to move that moose out of town." I told you they were smart guys. But how does one do that? They shot him. Don't cry or anything. They shot him with a tranquilizer dart. It was so cool. He just stood there, then he got real stoned . . . then he just fell over. The park rangers loaded him on a truck, drove out to the forest, set him free, the music played, the rangers waved good-bye and the moose lived happily ever after.

But the third rescue was especially moving. It involved a little deer, kind of like Bambi. White tail, little horns, you get the picture. This little deer was running crazy around a city park. Cars were crashing into each other. People were screaming. Mothers were running with their babies like this little deer was going to eat them or something. It was a little chaotic. Never fear, in came the park rangers.

Now, you can't trap a deer very easily, especially this little hyperactive deer. And apparently they didn't want to shoot him. So they came up with plan C. They decided to herd him into a corner of the park where there was a fence. If they could get him trapped against the fence, they could tackle him, put him in a truck and ship him out of town. Unfortunately, the deer had other ideas. In his little deer mind, all he thought was, "These guys in the green uniforms want to hurt me." So he ran . . . and ran . . . and ran.

Finally, he came to the fence. The park rangers had him surrounded. End of story, right? Wrong! The little deer freaked out. He started trying to jump the fence. Over and over he threw himself against the fence trying to escape. Eventually, his nose started bleeding and one of his horns broke off.

By this time I was really into it. I was screaming at the TV, "No, no, little deer. They are your friends. They want to take you to the forest where you can run and play and be with Bambi and Feline and Thumper and all of the forest animals."

(I told you I love this show.) By the time the rangers could grab him, he was beaten, bleeding and broken. Eventually, he died. The show ended with the rangers solemnly stating that they can't save all of the animals, especially those that don't want to be saved.

Now, why am I starting a book about family and parents with a story about some dumb animals? Simple. I think that many times, in many ways, we respond to God in the same way that that little deer reacted to the rangers.

We open up God's Word, the Bible. We listen to Christian teaching. We read or hear that God has guidelines, rules, plans, directions and commandments for our lives. And we panic. "Oh no, I could never do that. That could never work for me. That's too hard. God just wants to ruin my life." We panic . . . and we run. We look for an escape. We look for another way. We think that our situation is different. God just doesn't understand. We think we know better.

We do it in a lot of areas of our lives. Like sex and romance. We know what God says and thinks about purity. (Come on, admit it, we don't need any more sermons about waiting until marriage for sex.) We know the truth. We just want something else. So we run, questioning, "God, why are you trying to hurt me; why do you want to spoil my fun?"

We do it with substances. Be truthful . . . there is no one reading this book that thinks that putting illegal drugs into his body or getting drunk is a good thing. "Oh yeah, it was great, I puked so much I thought my lungs were going to come out . . . it was so cool." But we tell God to mind his own business, thinking something like this: "Quit telling me what to do; it's no big deal. I can handle this; my way is better."

We do it in lots of areas of our lives. But you know where I think we do it a lot? We do it with our parents. You've heard all of the verses—it's even one of the big Ten Commandments. Exodus 20:12 says:

> *"Honor your father and your mother, so that you may live long in the land the LORD your God is giving you."*

Or how about this one . . .

> *"Children, obey your parents in the Lord, for this is right. 'Honor your father and mother'—which is the first commandment with a promise—that it may go well with you and that you may enjoy long life on the earth"* *(Ephesians 6:1-3).*

And don't forget this one . . .

> *"Children, obey your parents in everything, for this pleases the Lord" (Colossians 3:20).*

And there are a bunch more in there that we'll get to later.

These are hard verses. Those are big words: honor . . . obey. Sometimes it's not so hard to honor and obey—other times it's really tough! And you know what we do when it's hard? We start acting like that weird little deer.

"Obey? No way. My parents don't understand. They aren't being reasonable. That's not fair. Nobody else's parents are as psycho as mine! There is no way that God wants me to . . ."

"Honor? You mean, if they deserve it, right . . . if they earn it, right? What about when they mess up? What about when they aren't Christians? What if they aren't very honorable people? Do you know what my dad did? Do you know what my mom said? Surely God doesn't expect me to . . ." Guess what? Yeah, he does. And that's a hard teaching. And the only way you are ever going to pull it off is with the power and strength of God's Spirit living in your life.

We're going to talk much more about this later but, not only does he command it, he also gives you a promise. When you follow his plan for your life with your parents, it will lead to two things. First, it will give you a better life (Exodus 20:12 and Ephesians 6:3) and second, you will please the Lord (Colossians 3:20). God doesn't just throw out flippant commands for no reason. He has a plan and like always, *his plan* brings us the awesome life he desires for us and it brings honor and glory to himself.

Chapter One

OK, back to "Wild Rescue." I was sitting on the couch trying to plead with that little deer to be reasonable, not to be afraid, that the rangers just wanted to help. And then I got hit with this really weird thought (that's pretty common for me, but this time, I think it was the Holy Spirit). What if the park rangers could speak "deer"? You know, like Dr. Doolittle? It would be so cool. The rangers could just walk up to the deer and say, "Hey, little deer, we are your friends. Don't be afraid. We are here to help. Just get on the truck with us and we'll take you to a great place, a place that was created just for you and you were created just for it. It's the life that you were meant for."

Then it hit me. That's exactly what God has done for us. See, I don't speak "God" very well, so God came to earth and spoke "man" in the form of his Son, Jesus Christ. And here is his message: "Hey, I am your friend. Don't be afraid. I'm here to help. Just walk with me and I'll take you to a great place, a place that was created for you and you were created for it. It's the life you were meant for."

Isn't that the life you want? God has an awesome plan for your life. As you read through these pages, don't be afraid. Some of it will be really hard to swallow. Some of it might make you mad. Some of it may seem so far out of reach that you'll never get there. Keep reading. Think about it. Pray about it. Let God teach you. I believe that if I, as the author, am faithful to God's Word, his Spirit will do the rest. Listen to his voice. Ask for his help.

This book is not about "How Your Parents Need to Change." It's about what God wants to do in *you*. And when he begins to work in you, amazing things will begin to happen in all areas of your life.

Getting Personal

1. *When I say, "God has a plan for your life," how does that make you feel? Worried? Comforted? Dreadful? Hopeful?*

2. *What are some areas of your life that you just kind of avoid talking about with God because you don't want to deal with them right now?*

3. *What is the hardest part about obeying your parents? Is it your problem? Is it their problem?*

4. *How can God promise that if you will honor and obey your parents, it will lead to a better life? It seems like it might lead to a harder, more controlled life. How could loss of independence be a positive thing?*

5. *What has God done to demonstrate to you that he can be trusted?*

6. *What do you think is God's overall goal for your life?*

7. *Why is this book not about "How Your Parents Need to Change"?*

two

The Brady Bunch,

the Partridge Family,

Joseph and Moses

Chapter Two

When I was a kid (don't you hate it when adults start a story with "when I was a kid"?), there were two TV shows that I couldn't miss each week. I rearranged my life to make sure that when these shows came on, I was sitting in my living room.

The first one was "The Brady Bunch." What a cool family. They lived in this huge, monster house with a lawn made out of Astroturf. Their dad used words like "groovy" and "far out" . . . and he drove a convertible. My dad drove an avocado green station wagon with wood panels on the side. Carol, the mom, was a babe (give me a break, it was the '70s . . . I was ten years old). Oh, get this, they had a maid, but their house was never dirty. There were six kids who shared one bathroom . . . and . . . they sang and danced on TV. Is that cool or what?

My other favorite show was "The Partridge Family." Talk about cool! The whole family sang together in a rock band and the mom drove a psychedelic school bus. It doesn't get any better than that.

But here was my favorite part about both of these families. Everything they did had a happy ending. Oh yeah, they had problems. I remember the time that Peter Brady's voice changed and Jan Brady had to get glasses. One time Keith

Partridge's hair didn't turn out right. But get this; all of their problems were solved in 30 minutes. By the time the show was over, everybody was laughing and hugging and singing. That's what I wanted my life to be like.

If you could design your whole life, what would it look like?
- *When and where would you be born?*
- *What would your parents be like, and how would they treat you?*
- *How would they treat each other?*
- *What would you look like?*
- *What kind of things would make you cry?*
- *What kind of friends would you have, and how would they treat you?*
- *What kind of natural abilities would you have— what would you be good at?*
- *What job would you have, and what income would you earn?*

Would it look anything like this? You would be born into slavery under an abusive, insecure dictator who murdered children when he felt threatened. Your parents, fearing for your life, would build a basket and float it down a crocodile-infested river and "trust God" that he would take care of you. You'd spend a few years of your life in wealth and then lose it all when you made one wrong move in anger—and you were even trying to do the right thing! One bad decision and the rest of your life would be changed in a moment. In one swift move, you'd go from being a "prince" to being a minimum-wage shepherd on the run from the law.

That's how a guy named Moses started his life. You know what I think? If Moses could have chosen his life for himself, it wouldn't have looked anything like that. But guess what? God used him to change the course of human history.

In this chapter, we are going to take a look at a couple of tough lessons. One you probably already know and don't like. The other may be new, and may sound rough at first, but in the end, it will be a great comfort. Here they are:

1. Most of your life is not under your control.

Great revelation, huh? Most of your life is not under your control. It is either under the control of other people or life circumstances over which you have little or no control. That might bother you at first but the more you think about it, the more you will realize that it's true.

Here's another example. You just read about Moses, but remember a few chapters earlier in the Bible? Genesis 37 tells the story of Joseph, the kid with the multicolored coat. Talk about a dysfunctional family! Joseph was one of the 12 sons of a guy named Israel (also named Jacob). Israel may have been a pretty important guy in the Bible, but he was kind of a jerk as a father. Read this:

> *"Now Israel loved Joseph more than any of his other sons, because he had been born to him in his old age; and he made a richly ornamented robe for him. When his brothers saw that their father loved him more than any of them, they hated him and could not speak a kind word to him" (Genesis 37:3, 4).*

Have you ever felt that your parents loved your brother or sister more than you? Isn't that an awful feeling? Joseph's brothers thought so. They hated the situation . . . and they hated Joseph . . . and when dad walked around the house handing out special presents to his "favorite," it didn't help the situation too much.

And Joseph, the 17-year-old smart mouth, didn't do much to help the situation either. One day, he announced to his brothers that he had two dreams where he was the king and his brothers bowed down to him. You know, even if it was true, that probably didn't help much. Here was dad's favorite, wearing his nice new coat proclaiming that one day he would be king and they would be his slaves. How would that make you feel? How about angry? How about so angry that you'd want to beat the tar out of Joseph, throw him down a well and sell him into slavery? Apparently, that's how they felt because that's exactly what they did (Genesis 37:5-29).

From that point on, Joseph began a wild ride in which his life was totally out of *his* own control. It included slavery, a false charge and conviction of attempted rape, which led to imprisonment and abandonment! We're not talking a 30-minute comedy show; we're talking about 17 years of life where Joseph had no choice in any of it. Other people and circumstances forced it all on him. He didn't agree to it, vote for it or like it. It was what he got, like it or not.

It's the same with you. Much of what happens in your life is not a matter of choice; it is forced upon you. Hold on. I'm not done. Second big lesson.

2. God is sovereign.

The word "sovereign" means that God has the power and ability to make anything he commands to happen. He can allow things that he hates to occur. And he has the power and ability to make them stop at his command. God could have forced Israel to be a better father. He could have zapped the family and turned them into the Brady Bunch. God had the ability to take away all of Joseph's problems. He could have stopped it with one great "poof." But you know what? He didn't.

He still has that ability. Abortion, adultery, homosexuality, drug abuse, AIDS, divorce, child abuse, cancer, heartache, starvation, betrayal, car wrecks. God is sovereign—he has the power to start or stop anything if he chooses to do so.

Question: Why? Why doesn't he make all of the bad stuff stop and allow only good things to happen?
Deep theological answer: I don't know!

If I were God:
- *Only "good" people would be allowed to be parents.*
- *There would be no abuse, no rape, no birth defects, no child abuse.*
- *People wouldn't have sex before marriage and would not want to get divorced after marriage.*
- *Everyone would have all of their material needs met, friends wouldn't leave or die and disease would disappear.*

But I'm not God . . . neither are you. In most of these areas of our lives, we don't get to choose.
- *Parents and family . . . we didn't get to choose.*
- *Pain, hurt, abuse . . . no choice.*
- *Health or physical abilities or disabilities. Oh, you can eat, exercise and wear your seat belt (and you should), but many times, it makes little difference.*

David said in Psalm 139:16:

Chapter Two

*"Like an open book, you watched me grow from con-
ception to birth; all the stages of my life were spread out
before you, the days of my life all prepared before I'd
even lived one day" (THE MESSAGE).*

In other words, sovereign, almighty God knew what was going
to happen to you every day of your life before you even took
your first breath. And in this huge knowledge that he has for
your life, he has one goal and reason for your whole exis-
tence—to be like Jesus.

Romans 8:28, 29 tells us:

"And we know that in <u>all</u> *things God works for the good
of those who love him, who have been called according to
his purpose. For those God foreknew he also predestined
to be conformed to the likeness of his Son, that he might
be the firstborn among many brothers."* (Emphasis mine.)

What's that mean? Simply put, God will use anything and all
things in your life to "conform" you to the image of Jesus. If
you are at point A and you need to get to point B, he knows
the best and only path to take you by and he will use *all*
things along the way in your life to make you like Jesus—*all*
things. ALL means ALL. Not just good things. Not just happy
things. Not just fun things. Not just churchy things. Not just
"religious" things. ALL means ALL.

Before you were born, he knew, one day you'd be hurt.
He knew the day you would be abused.
He saw the night that you cried over your parent's divorce.
He saw the times you would be betrayed before they happened.
He knew who would get drunk, get high and get pregnant.
In his book were written the times when you would break a law and hurt your parents.
He knew every sin you would commit before you were even born.

Now, let me be clear here. It is never God's will for you to sin or for someone to hurt or harm you. People have the free will to follow God's plans for them or to drastically depart from them. But because God is sovereign, they do so only because he allows it, which would sound kind of cruel and mean, unless two things were true.

1. He'd promise to go through it with you and protect you.

2. He'd promise to use it for a higher good.

Both statements are true. First Corinthians 10:13 says this:
   "But remember that the temptations that come into
   your life are no different from what others experience.

*"And God is faithful. He will keep the temptation from
becoming so strong that you can't stand up against it.
When you are tempted, he will show you a way out so
that you will not give in to it"* (NLT)

It's like this. We live in a world that is unfair, sinful and under
the control of Satan. We have no choice in this. But it's like
God has placed his hand around us, and we are inside his
grip, but every once in a while he chooses to spread his fingers and allow things to touch us. Satan wants to crush us, to
kill us—but God is in control and he won't let that happen. He
will either keep it away from you or he will support you so
that it won't crush you—or he may take you out of it!

Promise #1 from God:

He won't let anything in this world crush you.

Promise #2:

He will use all things for good and for his glory.

The only reason he chooses to spread his fingers and allow
you to be touched is for the highest purpose of conforming
you into the exact image of Jesus Christ. Picture it like this.
Have you ever had to go to the hardware store to have a key
copied? The sales clerk sticks your key in one side of a
machine called a key duplicator. In the other side, he places a
blank key. Then, he runs a guide down your master key. The

guide is connected to a spinning grinder. Whenever the guide moves into a groove in your master key, the grinder cuts and grinds an identical groove in the blank key. Sparks, dust and smoke fill the air. Now let's pretend that the blank key could talk (come on, go with it). What do you think the key would say? I think it would cry out, "Ouch . . . no . . . please stop . . . this hurts . . . why is this happening?" But the end result—an exact replica of the master.

Here we are in God's hand . . . he spreads his fingers . . . we cry . . . he protects and molds us into the image of Christ. God can use all those things that have "cut into your life" to make you more Christlike. Wow! What a plan!

I remember a few years ago in my ministry, I received a late-night call from Todd, one of the young men in my youth group. He was in tears. His parents had just announced to him that they were getting a divorce. You know, the "we still love you, but . . ." speech. Todd was crushed. He asked if I could come over. I left for his house immediately.

When I arrived, his tear-stained mother answered the door and pointed to Todd's room. When I opened the door, there was Todd, curled up on the floor crying. Sitting beside him crying and holding his hand was Jeremy, another boy from the youth group. I took it all in and understood in a moment. While I was about to give my youth ministry speech about trusting God and believing everything would be OK, Jeremy was ministering to Todd. His parents had dropped the same bomb on him a year earlier. He understood. God used Jeremy's situation to grind into him an experience that allowed him to empathize in ways I never could. Jeremy understood. He could cry the same tears because he had felt the same hurt.

Let me tell you two cool things about Jesus: First, he understands everything you will ever go through. He's been there, done it, felt it. He's experienced death, betrayal, disappointment, abuse, heartbreak, temptation and loneliness. Hebrews 4:15 assures us:

> *"For we do not have a high priest* [Jesus] *who is unable to sympathize with our weaknesses, but we have one who has been tempted in* <u>every way</u>, *just as we are—yet was without sin."* (Emphasis mine.)

He understands.

Secondly, he loves us more than we can comprehend. If you get nothing else out of this book, I hope you walk away knowing that God loves you. He proved it. Remember earlier, I said that God knew every sin you would commit even before you were born? Let me show you something even more amazing:

> *"But God demonstrates his own love for us in this: While we were still sinners, Christ died for us"* *(Romans 5:8).*

Even before we began to love him, follow him or change one thing about our lives, God had already provided for those future sins to be taken care of. God loves you. You have got to get that—he loves you! No matter how hard life feels, he won't let it crush you. He's taking care of you right now. His hand is around you right now. And even that thing in your life that seems so hard that you can see no purpose, no point and no hope—Sovereign God has got it under control.

There are no Brady Bunch families with 30-minute solutions. There are no Partridge families where life is one big party. There is just life, and life is hard. But more importantly, there is God—and he loves you and promises to take care of you.

Getting Personal

1. *If you could "design" your life, what things would and would it not include?*

2. *How does it make you feel when you hear, "Most of your life is not under your control"? Do you agree or disagree?*

3. *If you had been Joseph, how would you have felt in the middle of all the tough times he experienced? Abandoned? Unloved? Would you have questioned God?*

4. *What does "God is sovereign" mean?*

5. *If God is sovereign, how does that affect the way you see him and the way you see the circumstances of life?*

6. *What is the toughest thing in your life that you've had to live through so far?*

7. *Where was (is) God as you were (are) going through it?*

8. *How does God use "all things" to conform you into the image of Jesus?*

9. *Looking back, can you identify a time when God used your past experiences to help someone else and bring glory to Jesus Christ?*

Rules and Regulations

Chapter Three

What makes a parent a "good" parent? I mean, if you were to
create a job description for your parents, what is the first thing
you would want to put at the top of the list? A lot of things
might make the list. You might want them to be rich . . . or
beautiful. You might want them to be understanding . . . or
good listeners. You might want them to trust you, give you
privacy and give you freedom. You might want them to do and
be a lot of different things.

But at the top of the list, the first thing that you would
probably want would be . . . love. Good parents love their
children. I mean, they could be rich, good-looking, fun and
understanding, but if they didn't love you, it would all be
kind of meaningless.

Do your parents love you? Wow, big question. Well, do they?
How do you know? Your immediate response is probably,
"Yeah, of course they love me; they're my parents." OK, well,
how do you know? Because they say it? I say stuff all the time
I don't mean, don't you? So, how do you know that they really
love you?

Easy . . . they prove it by the things that they do. Jesus said
that our actions come from what's in our heart. He put it this
way in Luke 6:45:

"*A good person produces good deeds from a good heart, and an evil person produces evil deeds from an evil heart. Whatever is in your heart determines what you say*" (NLT).

James 2:18 tells us:
"*Now someone may argue, 'Some people have faith; others have good deeds.' I say, 'I can't see your faith if you don't have good deeds, but I will show you my faith through my good deeds'*" (NLT)

James is saying that if you believe something (in this case, in Jesus), it will cause you to do certain things in certain ways. Why do you do the things that you do? Because that's the condition of your heart. Because of the things that you believe. You say that your parents love you, or maybe you wonder if your parents love you. How do you know? And the answer is (drumroll, please) . . . they show it by the things that they do.

In my first book, *What's the Big Deal About Sex? Loving God's Way*, we spent some time looking for a biblical definition of love. Does love always give me what I want? Does love always make me happy? Does love always feel good? We find a great definition of love in the book of Ephesians. The apostle Paul explains to men what it means to love their wives, but this definition is by no means limited to romantic love. It applies especially well to families. Read with me:

*"In this same way, husbands ought to love their wives
as their own bodies. He who loves his wife loves himself.
After all, no one ever hated his own body, but he feeds
and cares for it, just as Christ does the church—for we
are members of his body" (Ephesians 5:28-30).*

Paul compares love for another person to the way a person
loves his own body. What do you do when you love your
body? You feed it and care for it. Think about it. Have you
ever gone out for an athletic team or decided to get into
shape? What did you do? Well, you probably started eating
differently. You provided your body with everything that it
needs. You may have started to eat healthy food, drink more
water, mix up protein shakes, take vitamin supplements, get
extra rest, study playbooks and strategies to become a better
player. You also took care that nothing came in and harmed
your body. Maybe you broke some bad habits such as smoking
or eating junk food. Depending on the sport, you may have
put on special equipment or pads to protect yourself. You did
whatever it took to give your body what it needs and protect it
from what could harm it.

Paul writes, "that's love." To feed and care for something, to
provide everything it needs and protect it from all that could
harm it. Do your parents try to do that? That's the definition
of love.

As a youth pastor, I have had too many conversations with students who sit and tell me, "My parents don't care what time I come in; my parents don't care who my friends are; my parents don't care what movies I see or what music I listen to; my parents don't care what kind of grades I get. . . ." And then, sometimes, right in the middle of a sentence, they stop with the phrase, "my parents don't care. . . ." It is an awful moment of realization.

See, parents who love, *do* certain things. They do whatever it takes to give you what you need and to protect you from harm. That doesn't mean that they lock you in a closet until you are 30, but it also doesn't mean that just because they love you, they let you do what you want.

When my two children were little, I walked them around the perimeter of our yard. I took them out to the front sidewalk and said, "This is the boundary. Don't go past this into the street." Then I walked them to the driveway on each side of our yard. "This is the boundary. Don't go into the neighbor's yard." Then I took them to the backyard. "This is the fence. Don't cross this boundary." Why would I do that? The answer? I loved them. Did they like it? Nope.

My son Jordan would look at the front street and, in his five-year-old mind, think that it was the perfect place to bounce a ball or ride a bike. Big, open, flat space. It made sense. But I knew that just down the street were some people who liked to drive way too fast. What kind of dad would I be if I just looked at Jordan and said, "Hey, I love you. Go for it. Hope you don't get hit by a truck"?

I knew that in one of our neighbors' yards, there was poison ivy. Alison is deathly allergic to poison ivy. I knew that our other neighbor didn't like us. "Jordan, don't go in that yard. He has a gun. He'll kill you." Behind our house lived the largest dog I've ever seen. It looked like a poodle on steroids. If Satan owned a dog, this was it. It didn't even bark. It just stood there and cussed at you. "Alison, don't go over the fence; he'll eat you." See, because I love my children, I put boundaries in place. I placed rules and regulations on their lives and consequences if they disobeyed.

Guys, why does your mom want to know where you are going, whom you are going with and what you are going to be doing? Because she loves you. She knows that there is no greater influence on your life than the people that you are hanging out with. She would be a negligent mom if she didn't ask.

Girls, why does your dad act overprotective when a guy shows interest in you or wants to take you out on a date? Because he loves you. I wouldn't loan my car out to many guys in my youth group. Why would I just turn my daughter over to some guy that I know nothing about? As a dad, I am first of all, a guy. I'm not accusing this guy of anything. I just understand more than you think I do. A good dad will do everything he can to make sure his daughter is safe and protected. By definition, that's what love does.

A few years ago, while on a mission trip to Kenya, my missionary friend, Peter Russell, told me a phenomenal story. Apparently, a few years earlier, a student had arrived from the States for a summer internship. After her 18-hour flight and seven-hour truck ride out to their home in the bush, the girl was suffering from some serious jet lag. The next morning, the missionaries told the girl to spend the day catching up on sleep and settling in while they were away for a day of ministry. After breakfast, the missionaries loaded the truck and waved good-bye until dinnertime that night. As the truck drove out of view, the young girl circled the house to the backyard and made her way to the "cho," the African version of an outhouse.

As she entered the cho, closed the door and took her seat, the floor of the outhouse chose that moment to give way and the girl tumbled 25 feet into the bottom of the hole. (Did I mention that this was a fairly well-used cho?) Because she was home alone, she would spend the next ten hours in the bottom of the hole, grasping the earthen sides to keep herself afloat. Late that night, the missionaries arrived home to hear the weak and pathetic voice of the intern as she cried out for help. (By the way, she went home the next day.)

Let me ask you this. How much money would it take to get you to jump down into that hole and spend the day? Ten dollars? One hundred dollars? One thousand dollars? Let me tell you something. You don't have enough money for me to volunteer to do that. But let me tell you something else. If one of my children fell down in there, you wouldn't have enough money to keep me out. What's the difference? Love. Love does whatever it takes to make sure that the thing loved is safe and secure.

Are your parents driving you crazy? Do you feel like you're playing "Twenty Questions" when you walk in the door or before you go out? Maybe you hear phrases like these constantly:

- *"Don't forget your curfew!"*
- *"Call when you get there and before you leave."*
- *"Sit up straight."*
- *"Don't use that tone of voice with me!"*
- *"That dress is too short and that shirt is too tight."*
- *"Don't talk with your mouth full!"*
- *"Pull your pants up."*
- *"You can do better than that."*
- *"You're grounded because of your grades."*
- *"Those are the rules."*

That's love. The alternative—"I don't care"—is much worse. Of course, the perfect example of this kind of love is found in Jesus Christ. Imagine, if you can, that every sin that you have ever committed had a smell, an odor, a stink. When you sinned (and we all do), you developed "spiritual B.O." What would you smell like? What if everyone had the same problem? What would this world smell like? I wonder if the whole place would smell like the bottom of an African cho.

I wonder what Heaven smells like. If sin "stinks," how awesome is the fragrance of Heaven? Who would ever want to leave Heaven to come and live among the stench of this sin-filled world? Guess who? Yep. Jesus. Philippians 2:5-8 describes the unbelievable step Jesus took to come and hang out with you:

"Think of yourselves the way Christ Jesus thought of himself. He had equal status with God but didn't think so much of himself that he had to cling to the advantages of that status no matter what. Not at all. When the time came, he set aside the privileges of deity and took on the status of a slave, became human! *Having become human, he stayed human. It was an incredibly humbling process. He didn't claim special privileges. Instead, he lived a selfless, obedient life and then died a selfless, obedient death—and the worst kind of death at that: a crucifixion" (THE MESSAGE).*

Why would he do that? You guessed it. Love. Love does whatever it takes to provide you with what you need and protect you from that which could harm you. You know what I've discovered about God and his rules? The only time he ever gives a command, a rule or a regulation that tells you not to do something is for one reason: He wants to give you something better. God never just spits out rules to spoil your fun. There is always a reason. Rules and regulations. That's good parenting. That's love.

Getting Personal

1. *If you could write your family's "parental job description," what things would it include? What would be the number one requirement?*

2. *How do your parents prove that they love you by what they do?*

3. *Based on Ephesians 5, what is the biblical definition of "love"?*

4. *How does love provide and protect?*

5. *What are some rules in your life that you don't really like? Be honest. Why are those rules in place?*

6. *How do love and rules go together?*

7. *Love does whatever it takes to provide and protect. How has Jesus done that for you?*

four

4

Why Obey?

Chapter Four

OK, time for another animal story. I was watching my nature channel the other night and guess what? It was shark week. May I just say, I love shark week! It doesn't get much better than a full week of shark shows. Anyway, I was watching this guy out on a boat and a TV reporter was interviewing him as he went about his business on his boat. The interview went something like this:

TV guy: May I ask what you are doing?

Shark guy: I'm pouring fish guts and blood into the water.

TV guy: Why would you do that?

Shark guy: I want to see if I can get sharks to come close to my boat. *(That sounded a little strange to me but hey, he's a shark guy, so I kept watching.)*

TV guy: What are you going to do when the sharks get here?

Shark guy: I'm going to jump into the water. *(OK, now I was getting a little worried.)*

TV guy: Why would you do that?

Shark guy: *(Honestly, this is what he said:)* I want to see if they'll *bite me.*

Now I was thinking that this guy was a complete idiot. What

was he thinking? Most people with more than two firing brain cells do all within their power to avoid being eaten by a shark. What in the world was this guy thinking? In my mind, he was nuts. It didn't make any sense.

Come to find out, the shark guy was testing a "shark suit" for the Navy. It was a specially-designed outfit that would protect a Navy pilot in the unfortunate event that he crashed in the ocean and a shark came looking for dinner. You know, a lot of the stuff I don't understand, I immediately label as wrong, crazy, stupid, insane. Why in the world should I do that?

Back to parents. OK, the love thing makes sense. Your parents love you so of course, they are going to do everything in their power to provide for you and to keep you safe. But honestly, sometimes their rules and regulations drive you crazy. What do you do when you don't understand your parents? What do you do when you don't like their rules?

Big answer: Obey anyway. That's probably not the answer you were looking for. You were hoping for something more like, "Tell them why their rules are stupid and why they have to change" or "If their rules make sense to you and don't inter-fere with your plans, then obey."

Sorry. When your parents lay down a rule for you, if you are a Christian you have only one option—obedience. Ephesians

6:1-3 says so:

> *"Children, obey your parents because you belong to the Lord, for this is the right thing to do. 'Honor your father and mother.' This is the first of the Ten Commandments that ends with a promise. And this is the promise: If you honor your father and mother, 'you will live a long life, full of blessing'"* (NLT).

Obeying your parents is always the right thing to do, unless they are asking you to do something that goes against God. In writing to the Christians, Paul realized that there would be some cases where a parent would actually demand that a child be involved in a sinful situation. The Bible is clear: God's Word always supersedes human authority. Upon being directed to stop talking about Jesus, Peter and the other apostles replied:

> *"'We must obey God rather than human authority'"* (Acts 5:29, NLT)

The only time God allows children to disobey their parents is to avoid sin. God never expects a child to participate in a sinful action at anyone's direction. Let me take this one step further. If you are the victim of sinful treatment or abuse, God isn't "doing this to you." It is not God's will for you to hang in there or tough it out. You need to get help immediately. Talk to a teacher, a pastor, a youth leader or a trusted adult. Your adult friend will make sure that you receive the protection you deserve and the help your parent needs as well.

But honestly, most of the times you want to disobey your parents have nothing to do with whether or not it is a sin. It has everything to do with whether or not you want to do it. Right? Think about it. What are most of the conflicts with your parents about? Obedience. They told you to do something or expected you to accomplish something and you didn't do it or argued with them about having to do it. Right?

- Home by 11:00? *Everyone else gets to stay out until midnight.*
- Clean my room? *It's my room, I like the smell.*
- Feed the dog? *I hate that dog!*
- Mow the yard? *What am I, the family slave?*

God was serious about this obedience thing. Check this out in the Old Testament:

"If a man has a stubborn and rebellious son who does not obey his father and mother and will not listen to them when they discipline him, his father and mother shall take hold of him and bring him to the elders at the gate of his town. They shall say to the elders, 'This son of ours is stubborn and rebellious. He will not obey us. He is a profligate [wow, big word—it means "broken character"] *and a drunkard.' Then all the men of his town shall stone him to death. You must purge the evil*

from among you. All Israel will hear of it and be afraid"
[yeah, I bet] *(Deuteronomy 21:18-21).*

Can you imagine going to school tomorrow?
    "Hey, where's Sally?"
    "Didn't you hear? Her mom shot her."
    "Why?"
    "Didn't unload the dishwasher."
    "Where's Jim?"
    "Dad ran over him with the car . . . bad grades."
You'd be running home, dusting and vacuuming, washing
windows.

Obviously God doesn't want our parents to literally kill us
when we disobey. Can you imagine the desperate situation of
a family where things are so bad at home that they finally
come to this point? I think God is illustrating that obedience
is a vital part of a godly man's and woman's life.

Why does God care so much about whether or not you obey
your parents? Is it that important to him that your room is
clean, your bed is made and your room is dust-free? Is he
standing in Heaven wringing his hands over the fact that you
didn't get your yard mowed? No, I'd say that those things
don't matter all that much to him. Then what's the big deal?

The *big deal* is this: God is more concerned about you and the person he is helping you to become. And get this: The number one force that he is going to use at this point in your life is your parents. Remember Romans 8:28, 29? God's goal for your life is to build into you all of the character and image of his Son, Jesus Christ. And he is using your parents to help mold you into what he desires.

God's Word says:
> *"Work hard and cheerfully at whatever you do, as though you were working for the Lord rather than for people"* *(Colossians 3:23, NLT).*

God is using your parents when they say, "Study hard, work up to your potential, do your best." God is not super concerned that you understand the wonders of algebra and calculus. He is more concerned that you are stretching and using the wonderful brain that he gave you. If you can learn to figure out difficult math problems, then he can trust you later to figure out some of life's difficult problems.

God's Word says:
> *"Work hard and become a leader; be lazy and become a slave"* *(Proverbs 12:24, NLT).*

God is using your parents when they say, "Get out of bed, help around the house, do your chores, get to work, you're acting lazy." God realizes that the person who is lazy is the person who winds up being a slave to debt and always in need.

In the parable of the talents, Jesus said:
> *"His master replied, 'Well done, good and faithful servant! You have been faithful with a few things; I will put you in charge of many things. Come and share your master's happiness!'" (Matthew 25:21).*

God is using your parents when they tell you to take care of your possessions, abide by a curfew, spend and save your money wisely and speak to others with respect. God knows that if you can be trusted and faithful with small things and situations now, he can entrust you with larger things later.

It always amazes me when I talk to a student who is totally frustrated by his parents' rules. He often says something like this: "I can't wait until I'm 18. I'm out of there. I am sick and tired of them telling me everything that I have to do. They are always on my case. They are always yelling at me and bossing me around."

I ask, "What are you going to do?" The response? "Join the Marines." Well, God will use a Basic Training drill sergeant for the same purpose . . . only the drill sergeant won't love you.

You know what I've discovered? God is pretty smart. (Wow, that was deep.) He knows that someday he is going to call you to do something. Command you to go somewhere or say something that is tough. He is going to tell you to live a life that is different from the lives of most of your friends. He is going to direct you to work out a difficult situation when most others would quit. He is going to command you to do something that in the world's eyes doesn't make much sense.

The reason God is so concerned with your obedience of your parents now in small things is to serve as basic training for obeying him later in big things. Read what Paul writes in describing you:

> *"For we are God's workmanship, created in Christ Jesus to do good works, which God prepared in advance for us to do" (Ephesians 2:10).*

The word "workmanship" can also be translated "masterpiece." Paul is saying that you are a work in progress. The ultimate goal is for you to become the person God wants you to be, one willing to be used for his glory. King David says in Psalm 138:8:

> *"The LORD will fulfill his purpose for me; your love, O LORD, endures forever—do not abandon the works of your hands."*

Remember the illustration in chapter two about the master key that was duplicated? You are that blank key in the duplicator, Jesus is the master key and your parents are one of the grinders God is using to fashion you into the image of the master. Does it hurt? Sometimes. Is it fun? Not always. Will you always understand? Not likely. Will you always agree? Definitely not. Is it worth it? Absolutely.

Getting Personal

1. *Here is a silly question: Has there ever been a time when your parents told you to do something that didn't make sense? What was it?*

2. *Why should you obey your parents when what they are telling you to do doesn't make sense?*

3. *When would God agree that the better thing to do would be to disobey your parents? Can you think of any specific examples?*

4. *Why is God so concerned about whether or not you obey your parents? Why is it such a big deal?*

5. How could obeying your parents today help you later in life?

6. How could obeying your parents influence your spiritual life?

7. Why does God refer to you in Ephesians 2:10 as his "master-piece"?

5

How to Light Your House

Chapter Five

Let's begin with a short English lesson. There is a term in grammar known as a metaphor. It is a tool used to compare one thing with another by speaking of it as if it were the other thing. For example, you might look at a guy and say, "He is a horse" or "He is an ox." Now, you are not saying, "I'm confused; I think that boy has literally turned into a big farm animal." You mean that he is really strong. You might say, "He is a pig." Literally speaking, he's not really a pig. You are saying that either he is proportioned similarly to a pig, he has bad eating habits or maybe, he stinks.

These are metaphors. One thing is spoken of as another. They are comparisons. They are not literal. But the idea is to look at the characteristics between the two things being compared and take note of their similarities. Sometimes they are good and sometimes they are bad.

She's an angel . . . he's a demon.
She sings like a bird . . . he is as mean as a snake.
She shines like the sun . . . he's as dumb as a rock.

Why the English lesson? Jesus taught one basic lesson over and over. It went something like this: "OK, you who claim to be my followers, you who say you love God and have accepted his forgiveness—on a daily basis, what difference does that make in your lives?" You see, every time that Jesus taught some deep truth like, "laying down your life for God," he always followed it with practical application. In essence he was saying, "This is how you do in real life what you say you believe in your head."

Have you noticed that a lot of people claim to love God, to be followers of Jesus, but you can't tell it in the way they live their lives? For a lot of people, the only way you would know that they claim to be Christians is that every Sunday they show up at a religious building. Jesus says to us, "If you say you believe—and it is the truth—it will make a difference in the way you live." And so, he illustrates this with two metaphors, he compares people to two things that illustrate how we are to live our lives *if* we really do claim to be followers of Jesus. The first thing he compares us to is salt. He said in Matthew 5:13:

> *"'You are the salt of the earth. But if the salt loses its saltiness, how can it be made salty again? It is no longer good for anything, except to be thrown out and trampled by men.'"*

Jesus says, "you are salt." Now, he's not literally saying you are composed of sodium chloride. He's saying, "Look at the attributes of salt and compare them to the attributes of your own life." When he taught, Jesus had the habit of looking at his crowd and using illustrations that he knew they would understand. When he talked to shepherds, he used sheep metaphors. When he spoke with fishermen, he used fishing metaphors. When he talked to farmers, he might talk about seeds.

In the time that Jesus was teaching, salt played a very important part in the lives of all of his listeners. To say the word "salt" immediately brought to their minds certain thoughts, and the comparisons were easy to make.

1. Salt brought to mind purity.

In ancient cultures, salt was thought to be a gift from Heaven because it came from two important sources—the sea and the sun. It was pure white in color and any imperfections immediately stood out and were removed. Salt was used in ceremonies where things were sacrificed up to God. Salt was the purifying agent of the sacrifice.

2. Salt was used as a preservative.

This was in the days before you ran to the grocery store, bought some meat, took it home and threw it in the freezer until you wanted it. In Jesus' day, you went to the market, picked out an animal, they killed it for you, you took it home, cut it up and buried it in a big barrel of salt.

Meat, if left alone, naturally begins to decompose and rot, especially in hot weather. Salt holds back the natural process of going bad. Once the salt is added, the meat will remain edible indefinitely (like those big country hams you see hanging in the grocery store). In the same way, salt can be used as medicine in right doses. Salt helps sores to heal. Have you ever gargled with salt water when you had a sore throat? Saline solution (salt water) is used as an antiseptic in washing out wounds.

3. Salt unlocks and brings out the natural flavor of food.

Salt has the power to take something that is kind of bland, kind of boring—and bring it to life. Too much salt overpowers, but measured in the right amounts, salt takes what is dull and makes it shine.

Jesus said, "You are salt." What was he saying? Let's take a closer look.

1. Salt is pure . . . are you?

The opposite of pure is impure, meaning that other things have crept in, corrupted and contaminated the element. God has a plan for an area of your life, yet many times the world around you creeps in and sells you another version, a cheaper version, an easier version, a more popular version, a version that makes you feel better. It is a wrong version, an impure version.

- *God says one thing about sex—the world says something different.*
- *God says one thing about your body—the world says something else.*
- *God says one thing about your family—the world says something opposite.*

2. Salt is a preservative . . . are you working in the same way in the world around you?

When things around you begin to fall apart, relationships are breaking up, people around you are wounded and hurting— what role do you play? Are you part of the cause for the pain or part of the healing agent?

You say, "Hey, we live in a rough world. I can't save everybody. I can't be nice to everybody. Some things are out of my control. Relationships fall apart." That's right, and meat naturally rots. Are you part of the problem or part of the solution?

3. Salt adds flavor . . . what flavor do you add?

The right amount of salt added to a certain food at the right time can make all the difference in the world. Similarly, if one person comes to another person at just the right time, it can be the difference between life and death. Words of healing, words of apology, words of encouragement. Helping someone who needs it simply because he needs it, not to get anything out of it. Just seasoning your world and making it better.

Remember these are metaphors; we're going to come back to them in just a minute and apply them to one very specific area of your life. Jesus goes on to say that not only are you salt, you are also light. Listen:

> *"You are the light of the world. A city on a hill cannot be hidden. Neither do people light a lamp and put it under a bowl. Instead they put it on its stand, and it gives light to everyone in the house. In the same way, let your light shine before men, that they may see your good deeds and praise your Father in heaven" (Matthew 5:14-16).*

In other places in the Bible, Jesus refers to himself as the light of the world, but here he says *we* are the light of the world. Is this a contradiction in the Bible? No, remember that Jesus is talking to people who claim to have God living in their hearts.

The idea is this: If Jesus, the light, lives in you, then that light becomes the light that you must shine before other people. This is a metaphor, so let's look at the attributes of light and draw some conclusions.

1. Light . . . meant to be seen, not hidden.

No one turns on a light and then hopes nobody sees it. The reason the light was turned on in the first place was to shine the light. One of the first songs little kids learn in church is, "This little light of mine, I'm gonna let it shine. . . . Hide it under a bushel? NO! I'm gonna let it shine!"

Question: Why did you turn on the light?
Answer: So I could see.

2. Light is meant to direct toward the right path and warn of dangers.

If you were to go to downtown Louisville, Kentucky, and look at the Ohio River, you would see different-colored lights up and down the river. To the pilots of ships, these are called navigation lights and they mark out the channels in the river where it is safe to sail. If the captain ignores these lights, he risks running aground or hitting some unseen obstacle below the water.

The same thing is true at the airport. Each of the colored lights means something to the pilots of the airplanes. This runway is safe . . . this one is for landing . . . this one is for taxiing . . . this one is for taking off. If a pilot ignores the lights, disaster will follow.

Jesus said, "You are the light of the world." What did he mean?

1. Lights are meant to shine, not be hidden.

Hidden lights are useless. If you claim to be a Christian, yet it seems like you spend most of your time trying to overcome that title or your actions seem to deny it, maybe you just like the idea of having God's light inside of you. You like having your sins forgiven, the thought of going to Heaven and having God help you through your life. But perhaps you've never really had the light. Worth thinking about.

2. Lights direct and help others find safety and warn of danger.

Do you do that? Are you making others' lives better? When it comes time to make a decision about something that is right or wrong, do you speak up or are you part of the problem? I don't know how many times I got in trouble in high school with a group of friends because nobody spoke up and said, "This isn't a good idea. This is wrong. Let's do something else." What kind of light are you?

Jesus said you are the salt of the earth and the light of the world. He didn't say you are the salt of the church and the light of the youth group. Christian beliefs that you acknowledge in youth group and then discard the moment that the lights come on and you leave are useless. They are worthless. The one group of people that God promises not to have anything to do with are those who pretend to know him but don't really act like it. Check out these hard-hitting verses:

> "Knowing the correct password—saying 'Master, Master,' for instance—isn't going to get you anywhere with me. What is required is serious obedience—doing what my Father wills. I can see it now—at the Final Judgment thousands strutting up to me and saying, 'Master, we preached the Message, we bashed the demons, our God-sponsored projects had everyone talking.' And do you know what I am going to say? 'You missed the boat. All you did was use me to make yourselves important. You don't impress me one bit. You're out of here'" (Matthew 7:21-23, THE MESSAGE).

So, what does this salt and light lesson mean for your life? We could apply it to any area. Your sex and dating life, your relationships with your friends, the way you treat different people and situations at school. But, guess what? Let's take a look at the one place where it is sometimes the most difficult to follow Jesus Christ—your home.

Many Christians seem to think that all of the directions that Jesus gave apply to every place but home. I get calls from parents all the time that go something like this: "I know Johnny has gone on mission trips, and attends Bible studies and retreats, but you should see him at home! Sometimes he comes in from church and it's like Jekyll and Hyde. One minute, he's an angel and the next, he's the spawn of Hell! What's the problem?" The problem is that we don't understand that being the salt of the earth and the light of the world needs to start at home. You are the salt of your home and the light of your family. What do I mean?

1. Salt is pure and uncontaminated.

Listen, the world around you has a cheap definition of the family. I challenge you to find one TV show or movie in which the parents are portrayed as wise, understanding or clued in. In most shows I've seen, the message is clear: "Blow off your parents. Obey them if it suits you. They are the enemy. Lie to them, don't tell them about your life, don't communicate, treat them however you feel, wipe your feet on them, take advantage of them. You didn't ask to be born; they owe you. Point out their faults, their mistakes, throw their words back in their faces, forget about their problems, their pressures, their feelings, their pain and their needs."

But the Bible has a different plan. God says, "Unless your parents are telling you to disobey me, honor and respect them." TV will never tell you to do that. Music will tell you to make your own decisions, to follow your heart. But let me ask you this: If you are supposed to obey your parents only when you agree with them or understand why they are telling you to do something when it's fun or easy, how are you going to react when God tells you to do something hard, something you don't understand? Probably you'll react in the same way that you treated your family.

2. Salt preserves and makes things better.

Let me make one thing very clear. You can't change your parents, and you are not responsible for their actions—but you are responsible to God for how you dealt with your circumstances. If you are in an abusive or dangerous situation, remember God certainly doesn't expect you to "stick it out" or "make the best of it." But let's face it, most of the problems which go on in your house are partially your fault. Families are sometimes going to disagree, stress out and have conflict—

but the real question is this: Are you making the situation harder or better?

Are you part of the problem or part of the solution? Jesus says that if you are a follower of his, you'll do your best to make it better.

- *You be honest . . . even if it means consequences.*
- *You keep your word . . . even if it means sacrifice.*
- *You apologize . . . even if it means swallowing your pride.*
- *You forgive . . . not because they deserve it, but because you don't deserve it and God keeps on forgiving you.*

You do your part to be the salt of your family.

3. Light is meant to shine.

The place to start living out your love for God is at home. Yet the people at home are the ones who rarely get to see our little mission trip good works. It's amazing! I'll take students to some third-world country and they will spend eight hours a day laying cement block, running wheelbarrows full of sand up a hill, wiping snotty little noses of poor mountain children, eating nothing but peanut butter and jelly and tuna sandwiches for a week—and they love it. The tougher, the better. Cold showers, no problem. Cuts and blisters, bring them on. Bugs in the food, cool!

But at home, these same students gripe and complain if supper isn't an exciting adventure. They don't understand that the trash probably needs to go out every day. And how dare their moms expect them to make the bed, do laundry and adhere to a curfew? So they don't hesitate to share with the family that this isn't the way it should be. Listen, Christianity needs to start at home before you get on an airplane and go off to save the world.

4. Lights direct toward the right path and warn of danger.

Every once in a while, I get little cards telling me that I'm a good youth minister or that I taught a good lesson. Sometimes I receive thank-you notes for taking students on a trip. Those are really encouraging to me; they mean a lot. I even have a special folder I keep them in. Sometimes I leave them taped to the door of my office for weeks at a time. But as much as those mean to me, they don't even come close to compliments I receive from my two kids or my wife.

One whole wall of my office is dedicated to notes and pictures from my family. You know why? I like them better than I like all the people I minister to. (I hope that doesn't hurt anyone's feelings.) People can tell me that I'm a good youth minister. My boss can tell me that I'm a good employee. That will really make my day. But if Alison tells me that I'm a good dad, if Jordan makes something for me or if Robin sticks a card in the bottom of my suitcase when I'm leaving for a trip—that makes my life.

I believe that today, with just one or two sentences you could begin to totally change the atmosphere of your home. How? Little things. Leave a note on your parents' bathroom mirror. Stick a card in your mom or dad's briefcase. You might be asking right now, "But what would I say?" Little things. Like, "I just haven't told you lately, but you're a great mom," or "Thanks for driving me everywhere" or "Dad, thanks for all you do for me."

You might be thinking, "That's really queer." OK, what's the alternative? Keep moving apart? Let your boat run aground? Let me ask you: What is one thing you could do or say, even tonight, to let God's light shine at your house? What are you waiting for? Just maybe God is calling you to do it.

Getting Personal

1. *What does this statement mean to you: "If you really believe in Jesus, it will make a difference in your life"?*

2. *Jesus compared you to salt: it's pure, it's a preservative, it brings flavor. In what ways are you to be like salt?*

3. *Jesus compared you to light: light shines and warns others of danger. How are you supposed to function as light?*

4. *What does this statement mean to you: "You can't change your parents, but you are responsible for your response to your circumstances"?*

5. *Are you more part of the problem or part of the solution to some of the problems in your home?*

6. *If you were to do your part as a healing agent, what are some things you would need to change in your own life?*

7. *What do you know God is telling you to do right now?*

The Trust Factor

Chapter Six

Recently, I polled several hundred high-school students in regard to what was the biggest area of conflict between their parents and them. By far, it came down to one word: trust. I hear statements like these all the time: "My parents don't trust me. My parents are too strict. They treat me like a baby. They don't let me make my own decisions. I'm not a little kid anymore. Why don't they trust me?"

Trust. It's a huge thing. We all want people to trust us. Especially people we look up to. The problem is that we sometimes make an incorrect assumption. Here it is: "If you loved me, you would trust me." Is that true? Do love and trust go hand in hand? If you love someone, should that lead to automatic trust that he or she will do the right thing? If you don't trust someone, does that mean that you don't love that person?

Well, I hate to keep beating the same drum, but let's go back to the biblical definition of love. What does love do? According to Ephesians 5:29, it provides and protects. In other words, if I love you, I will do all within my power to provide you with what you need and protect you from that which will harm you. Let me illustrate. When my son Jordan was a little kid, Robin and I gave him a brand-new shiny bike for Christmas. Why? Why would I buy my son a bike? That's easy. As a father, I like to provide good gifts for my children. I wanted to see his delight on Christmas morning. I loved the sound of his squeal as he ran over to the tree. I knew that his days on his Big Wheel were about over and he was ready for a step up in transportation.

I love Jordan. So I did the natural thing. I sat him on his new bike, wished him luck and gave him a big shove into the street and went inside, right? Wrong! Learning to ride a bike was a long process at our house. First of all, along with the bike came a really smart thing called training wheels. I stayed up almost all night on Christmas Eve assembling this bike and making sure that the training wheels attached to the back wheel were locked on tight and secure. Not only that, but Robin had carefully picked out a helmet for Jordan to wear. Before Jordan's backside ever touched the bicycle seat, his topside was securely buckled into a U.S. Bicycle Association-approved safety helmet.

Why? Why would I do that? Didn't I love Jordan? Absolutely. So why would I insist on the training wheels and the three inches of plastic and Styrofoam buckled to his head? Didn't I trust him? Please read my answer carefully . . . NO! No, I didn't trust him. He was five years old. He had never been on a bike of this size in his life. And I wasn't done. We had rules about when he could ride his bike. Robin or I had to be outside with him. We had limits concerning where he could ride his bike. At first, it was our driveway, later the sidewalk, eventually the street in front of our house. It would be several years before his first solo run around the block.

What kind of dad does that make me? Overprotective? Paranoid? How about, by definition . . . loving. See, I love my son. Therefore I am going to do everything in my power to not only provide him with what he needs, but also to protect him from what might hurt him. I can hear you saying, "But Jim, if you loved him, you should have enough confidence in him to trust him to make the right decisions." Let me respond as politely as possible. That's a bunch of baloney!

I had total trust in Jordan that *someday* he would be a great bicycle rider. I had zero trust in his present ability. That would only come with time, experience and proof. Do you see where I'm going with this? Trust isn't something that automatically comes with love. Trust is built over time through experience and proof. Jesus taught the same thing about trust. Read this story that he told in Matthew 25:14-18:

> *"Again, it will be like a man going on a journey, who called his servants and <u>entrusted</u> his property to them. To one he gave five talents of money, to another two talents, and to another one talent, each according to his ability. Then he went on his journey. The man who had received the five talents went at once and put his money to work and gained five more. So also, the one with the*

"two talents gained two more. But the man who had received the one talent went off, dug a hole in the ground and hid his master's money.'" (Emphasis mine.)

Are you following the story? Apparently, this rich guy was leaving town for a while and *entrusting* (root word—trust) a few talents (in Bible times, that was an amount of money) to each of his servants. Let's continue reading in Matthew 25:19-29:

"After a long time the master of those servants returned and settled accounts with them. The man who had received the five talents brought the other five. 'Master,' he said, 'you <u>entrusted</u> *me with five talents. See, I have gained five more.'*

"His master replied, 'Well done, good and faithful servant! You have been <u>faithful</u> *with a few things; I will put you in charge of many things. Come and share your master's happiness!'*

"The man with the two talents also came. 'Master,' he said, 'you <u>entrusted</u> *me with two talents; see, I have gained two more.'*

"His master replied, 'Well done, good and faithful servant! You have been <u>faithful</u> *with a few things; I will put you in charge of many things. Come and share your master's happiness!'*

"Then the man who had received the one talent came. 'Master,' he said, 'I knew that you are a hard man, harvesting where you have not sown and gathering where

"you have not scattered seed. So I was afraid and went out and hid your talent in the ground. See, here is what belongs to you.'

"His master replied, 'You wicked, lazy servant! So you knew that I harvest where I have not sown and gather where I have not scattered seed? Well then, you should have put my money on deposit with the bankers, so that when I returned I would have received it back with interest.

"'Take the talent from him and give it to the one who has the ten talents. For everyone who has will be given more, and he will have an abundance. Whoever does not have, even what he has will be taken from him.'" (Emphasis mine.)

Did you get it? The rich guy came back and found that two of his servants had taken the little bit of responsibility he had given them and did great. They had doubled his money. And what was their reward? More responsibility. They had proven over time that they could be trusted. But don't forget servant number three. He couldn't handle even a little responsibility and ended up losing it all.

So, what does this story have to do with riding a bike or your parents trusting you? Simple. As a father, I wanted my son to succeed as a bike rider. The master in Jesus' parable wanted his servants to succeed in business. Your parents, believe it or not, have the goal that one day you will be able to make mature, wise and trustworthy decisions. How are you going to achieve that goal? Respond like the first and second servants in the story. Be *faithful* in a few things and see what happens. As you succeed in the small things, more and more responsibility and trust will be given.

And the opposite is true as well. "'Whoever does not have, even what he has will be taken from him.'" Jesus is saying if you can't handle the small stuff, there's no way you can be trusted with the big stuff.

Do you remember the student survey I mentioned at the beginning of this chapter, regarding their parents' strictness and lack of trust? Here is one other thing that is interesting. In that same survey, most of the high-school students revealed that they would be at least as strict, if not more strict, with their own children. In other words, they were saying, "I want my parents to trust me more, but, if I were them, I wouldn't."

The truth is that it is a big, bad world out there and we all need some training wheels and helmets in our lives. Right now, your parents play that role. Those training wheels and helmets are things like curfews, rules, expectations, chores and responsibilities. The goal? Maturity. To prepare you for going "solo" around the block. It's called trust, and it only comes through time, experience and proof!

Getting Personal

1. *Why is the phrase, "If you loved me, you'd trust me" not necessarily true?*

2. *As a parent, why would I insist that my five-year-old son wear a safety helmet when riding his bike? If I loved him, wouldn't I allow him to make his own decisions?*

3. *Be honest. If your parents said, "Hey, we trust you; do whatever you want," do you think you would get into more trouble or less trouble?*

4. *What are some of your parents' rules that have saved you from some big problems, temptations or bad situations?*

5. *How does faithfulness in small things lead to trust with larger things?*

6. When you become a parent, do you think you will be more lenient or stricter than your parents? Why?

7. Knowing what you know about yourself, should your parents be more or less strict with you?

seven

7

Trust . . . How Do I Get It?

Chapter Seven

OK, so if maturity is the goal and trust is something that you build, how do you build it? Where do you start? Great question. Read this:

> *"Consider it pure joy, my brothers, whenever you face trials of many kinds, because you know that the testing of your faith develops perseverance. Perseverance must finish its work so that you may be mature and complete, not lacking anything"* (James 1:2-4).

James is saying that God's goal for you is the same as what we have been talking about—maturity. What is God's plan for maturing you? Trials of many kinds that test your faith. Faith is another word for trust. A tested faith develops perseverance. Perseverance is another word for the ability to keep going. And the result of perseverance is . . . maturity.

Let me see if I can illustrate this. Let's say that you have a goal of being able to bench-press 300 pounds. So you go to the gym, load 300 pounds on the bar and give it a try. If you are like most of us, someone had better be close by ready to call 911. It's ridiculous for someone who has never lifted weights to even attempt such an ominous weight.

Let's say that you survived your 300-pound suicide attempt, sat down with a trainer and began to make a plan to reach your goal. The trainer would probably first try to identify your present level of strength. Let's say that you can bench-press 150 pounds pretty comfortably. The trainer would then devise a plan so that slowly, over time, more and more weight could be added to the bar until eventually, you would reach your goal.

We tried this earlier with the key duplicator. Let's try it with your muscles. Let's suppose that the muscles could talk. You bench-press 150 pounds and your muscles say, "No problem, we can handle that." But now, you add ten extra pounds to the bar. Your muscles now say, "Uh oh. What's happening? This hurts. Ouch, we're sore. If this guy is going to do this to us, we'd better be prepared for the next time." So the muscles grab some protein and build themselves up a little bigger. A few days later, your muscles are saying, "160 pounds? No problem, we can handle that." So you add ten more and the process starts all over. Eventually, the goal is for your muscles to say, "300 pounds? No problem, we can handle that."

That's the goal—maturity. For the weight lifter, that might be 300 pounds. For you, the more trust you can build, the closer to the goal of maturity you will be. Each test you face, each time you are stretched, each trial you survive and overcome—you have added a little more weight on the bar on the way to achieving your goal. Let's take a look at a few ways you can begin to build trust on your journey to maturity.

1. The goal is maturity, not getting your own way.

If you go into this thing with this attitude, "If I do these three things, then my parents will let me do what I want," then you have missed the point. Yes, if you are mature, you probably will get to have more control over your own decisions, but that is the result, not the goal. The goal is for you to have the maturity to make those decisions. You have to approach this trust-building thing with the attitude that God is going to do something good in your life, even if it hurts. Proverbs 3:11, 12 says:

> *"But don't, dear friend, resent GOD's discipline; don't sulk under his loving correction. It's the child he loves that GOD corrects; a father's delight is behind all this"* *(THE MESSAGE).*

The writer here makes a great comparison between a parent and the Lord. Both discipline and correct because of love. If you are going to get serious about allowing God to build maturity in your life, then you have to trust that God is in control and is using circumstances and trials in your life for your good. Remember, he's sovereign. You are also going to have to throw out timelines. If God really is in control, then he will bring you what you need at just the right time.

2. Start with the small stuff.

Jesus said in the parable of the talents (Matthew 25) that the person who could be trusted with the small stuff would eventually be entrusted with much greater responsibility. The person who couldn't handle the small stuff would never be given the opportunity for greater trust.

A few days ago, my son Jordan asked me if he could have a puppy . . . not just any puppy—a big puppy—one that would eventually grow into a big dog. Now, I've always had big dogs, so I am a big fan of big dogs. But I also know that big responsibilities come with big dogs. And we had a problem. We already have a little dog. His name is Cody. He's a pug and I think he might possibly be the ugliest dog I've ever seen. He's . . . how can I say it and be kind? Challenged. Cody is infamous for his loud snoring and revolting odors. Every day, a civil war erupts in our home over whose turn it is to feed, water or walk Cody. Don't misunderstand me. We all love Cody. Jordan was just ready for a little "cooler" model of dog.

Jordan and I sat down and made a list of responsibilities that he would have to fulfill in order to prove he was mature enough to handle the care a big dog would require. That began with taking care of the dog we now had without being asked or told. It included making his bed each morning, picking up his dirty clothes and finishing his homework in a timely manner. If he could demonstrate responsibility in these areas, then possibly, he would be ready to assume a greater level of responsibility at a later time.

The way to receive trust in the big things is to prove you are trustworthy in the little things. What do I mean?
- *Obey your curfew.*
- *Clean up your room.*
- *Take care of your possessions.*
- *Do your best on your homework.*
- *Do your chores around the house without being reminded (or threatened).*
- *Obey your parents the first time they direct you.*
- *Go the extra mile.*

Ever wonder where that "go the extra mile" saying came from? Well, it originated with Jesus himself. Take a look at what he said in Matthew 5:41:

> *"'If someone forces you to go one mile, go with him two miles.'"*

Jesus was in the middle of a sermon about how to deal with those in authority over you (in this case, the Romans, who were the enemy of the Jews). Jesus referred to a Roman law, which allowed a Roman soldier to stop any Jewish citizen on the street, and command him to carry his possessions. By law, the citizen was required to carry the burden one mile, and then he was free to go. Essentially, Jesus was telling his followers, "You obey the soldier and carry it the required mile. Then, voluntarily carry it a second mile."

Can you imagine the gasp that went through the crowd? "Second mile? Volunteer? Why would we do that? We hate the Romans." Why would Jesus command us to do such a thing? Isn't it enough that we just obey? Well, yes, simply obeying is probably "just enough." But remember, the goal isn't just to do enough—to get by. The goal is maturity.

Jesus knew that if you were mature enough to go the second mile, those watching would "'see your good deeds and praise your Father in heaven'" (Matthew 5:16). You know what usually happens when your parents see you not only act responsibly in the small things, but also go the extra mile? They begin to think of you as mature. You know what one of the results of maturity is? More trust. You know what one of the benefits of trust is? More freedom.

3. Make good decisions.

I used to think that if a person had courage, he would never be afraid. Over the years, I've realized that courage doesn't mean lack of fear. Courage means that a person still does the right thing in spite of his fears. I've discovered the same thing about maturity. Maturity is not the ability to handle every situation that comes your way. Maturity is the ability to admit that you cannot handle every situation but you take the necessary precautions to make sure the right thing gets done anyway.

For example, if you are a mature, Christian young man, you should be able to be trusted alone in a house with a mature, Christian young woman. Right? WRONG! I can't tell you how many young couples I have counseled who thought they could "handle it" but things "just happened." I'm not saying that you are a pervert or some stalker. On the contrary, I'm saying that you are a normal, healthy, Christian, red-blooded young man. But a *mature*, normal, healthy, Christian, red-blooded young man realizes that it is foolish to put himself into a tempting situation.

Or suppose you are at a party that starts pretty innocently but takes a turn for the worse. Chaperones are nonexistent. Alcohol or drugs make their appearance. Tempers begin to flare. Couples begin to pair off for some "one on one" time. What do you do? Ignore it? Pretend it isn't happening? Keep your nose out of it as long as it doesn't affect you? What's the mature thing to do?

First of all, don't try the line, "I'll stay there and be a good witness." Bad idea. Yeah, everyone needs a designated driver. Yeah, I guess there is a small chance that someone at the party is going to see you and say, "Hey, Jim's not drinking . . . let's all stop too." But nine times out of ten, you are either going to cave under pressure and compromise your standards, or at best, those around you or those who heard that you were there are going to assume that you partied like everyone else. Paul said it best in 1 Corinthians 15:33:

> *"Do not be misled: 'Bad company corrupts good character.'"*

Don't fool yourself. You are more likely to be pulled down rather than to pull anyone up at the party. What's the mature thing to do? Simple . . . get out. Call your parents. Call your youth pastor. Call someone to come and get you. Notice, I said "simple"; I didn't say "easy." Doing the mature thing is rarely easy. That's why immature people can't do it. Maturity is the ability to do the right thing in spite of the circumstances. Maturity doesn't mean that you can handle every situation. Maturity means that you realize that you *can't*, so you take the necessary steps to avoid the situation in the first place—or you get out if you find yourself in that predicament.

4. Consistency is the key.

Earlier in the chapter, I stated that you needed to throw out any timeline by which you should expect trust to be given. That's different for each one of us. But while there isn't a set time for gaining trust, there is a set number for blowing trust. One. In one moment, you can blow what took years to build up.

For example, have you ever made a concerted effort to watch your language or your humor? But then, just once, you made a mistake and said something that you shouldn't have? What is the one thing that everyone points out to you? Yep. "Remember that one time when you said . . . ?" I hate that, but that's how people often are. You might do 50 things right, but if you do one thing wrong, that's what people tend to remember.

It's the same with parents and trust. The only way to build trust is consistency. And if you blow it, it's going to take quite a while to rebuild it. It doesn't matter if it was a mistake. It doesn't matter if you're really sorry. The only thing that can build back trust is time. Think about it. If I came up to you and said, "Hey, I haven't had a wreck in three days—can I borrow your new car?", you'd tell me to get lost. If you came up to me and said, "Hey, Mr. Burgen, can I take your daughter out? I'm sexually pure 50% of the time," I'd tell you in pretty certain terms that your life was in danger if you didn't get out of my face in about three seconds.

See, there are no shortcuts. The only way to build trust is time. The more mature decisions you make in a row, the greater trust you will earn. If you make a mistake, it is going to take a longer time to gain it back. So remember: Maturity is the goal. It starts with the small stuff. It involves making good, wise, mature decisions. And it takes time.

Getting Personal

1. What is God's primary plan to grow you to maturity?

2. How do "trials of many kinds" accomplish maturity in your life?

3. Why is maturity a better goal than getting your own way?

4. Why does maturity mean "going the extra mile"?

5. How does maturity lead to more trust?

6. *How does more trust lead to more freedom?*

7. *How are the decisions you make a measure of your level of maturity?*

8. *What is the natural result of breaking trust? How do you get it back?*

Working Out Problems

Chapter Eight

Let's begin with a couple of scenarios. Imagine that a bunch of your friends are getting together for some fun this Friday night. Probably rent some movies, eat some pizza and just hang out. You ask your parents. They say, "No, you've been out enough this week. You need to stay home." You think it's ridiculous. Everyone else's parents are letting them go. Your parents don't even have plans for you. They just want you to stay home. What do you do?

Or how about this, girls? You really like this guy and he finally asks you out. You tell your parents that you're going out this Friday night. They say, "Nope, not until we meet him first and get to know him a little better." You are furious. How embarrassing. How old-fashioned. What do you do?

Or how about this one? You made a mistake, you were grounded, you're really sorry, but now, something "important" has come up and you really want to do it. But your parents inform you that you are still grounded and you can't go.

Now, if you were a "real Christian," you and your parents would never disagree, right? Wrong. There will probably be many situations in which you and your parents are going to disagree. You want to go somewhere . . . they say, "No." You want to drive . . . they say, "Not now." You want to do something . . . they say, "You can't."

Disagreement is inevitable. Even the most loving family is going to have times when two differing opinions collide with one another. Because of the way God wired us, when we are faced with conflict, our natural emotional response is frustration, sadness or even anger. These responses are not necessarily bad. The real issue is how we choose to act in the face of these emotions. What are you supposed to do when you really disagree with what your parents are telling you to do? How are you supposed to respond to your parents when what they are doing or saying is making you angry?

1. Don't sin in anger.

In Ephesians 4:26, 27 the apostle Paul instructs us:
> *"'In your anger do not sin': Do not let the sun go down while you are still angry, and do not give the devil a foothold."*

Notice what the Bible is *not* saying here. It is not saying that it is a sin to *be* angry. It is saying that *when* you are angry, don't sin. Verse 27 implies that when a person is angry, the devil may try to use this anger as a "foothold" or starting place to mess up your life even more. Think about it. When are you most likely to say something that you shouldn't? When you are mad. How many times have you gotten all fired up about something? Maybe somebody said something to you and it really made you mad. Maybe you heard something or someone got in your face and ticked you off—and before you knew it, you said something or did something that you normally wouldn't do.

My senior minister, Bob Russell, told me the story about playing golf with his brother when they were younger. All day long, Bob had been hitting pretty bad shots, so he was already really frustrated. His brother, John, took the opportunity to point out the bad shots with a snicker in his voice. Finally, Bob had had enough, so he teed up the ball and drove it right in the direction of his brother. (I know it doesn't sound very spiritual for a senior minister.) Have you ever done something or said something—you knew you shouldn't but you did it anyway—and as soon as you did it, you wished you could reach out and take it back, but you couldn't. Well, this was one of those moments. Luckily, John ducked at just the right moment and avoided being decapitated by a killer golf ball.

Sometimes when we are angry, we do and say some pretty stupid stuff. Sometimes we use language we normally wouldn't use. Some of us might even lose control and hit things, break things, slam things or throw things. Why? Because in our anger, we have allowed sin to come in and take control. Proverbs 29:11 gives this advice:
> *"A fool gives full vent to his anger, but a wise man*

keeps himself under control."

Galatians 5:22, 23 describes the lifestyle of a follower of
Christ:
> *"But when the Holy Spirit controls our lives, he will
> produce this kind of fruit in us: love, joy, peace,
> patience, kindness, goodness, faithfulness, gentleness,
> and* <u>self-control</u>. *Here there is no conflict with the law"*
> (NLT, emphasis mine).

Guess what one of the signs of spiritual maturity is? Yep, self-
control. Of course there are going to be times when you get
angry—even with those you love. But the mature person is
able to maintain control in spite of anger.

What does that mean? It means you keep a respectful and
honorable tone and volume with your parents. It means you
don't use inappropriate language when expressing your
thoughts and feelings. It means you don't gossip about what
goes on at your house or belittle your parents with all of your
friends. It means that even though you are angry, you don't
lose control and throw a childish tantrum.

It is amazing to see so many students who are active in their
churches and youth groups: memorizing Scripture, going on
retreats, lifting their hands in worship, going on mission
trips—but when they get home, it's like Dr. Jekyll and Mr.

Hyde. They treat their parents like dirt. It's scary the way some Christian students talk to their parents. It's as if Christianity applies to every situation . . . except your home. Maybe you are tempted to think, "I don't have to be a Christian at home."

Wrong. That's where it needs to start. Before you go off saving your school or flying off to some foreign country, maybe you need to work on your witness right in your own house. Whoops . . . that was a little sermon. Sorry. Back to the subject of anger. Everybody is going to get angry sometimes. What we do when we are angry has to be kept in check. Satan is just waiting to jump on the opportunity.

2. Is God trying to tell me something?

Remember that God uses all things in your life, including your parents, to build things into your life. And, remember that God is sovereign, meaning he determines what does and doesn't happen. Could it be that whenever you and your parents come to a disagreement, that maybe God is trying to tell you something? Could it be that maybe, just maybe, the reason that your parents won't let you do something is because God doesn't want you to do it either?

Maybe God is using your parents to keep you from filling your mind with what he knows is in that movie or at that concert. Maybe God is using your parents to keep you away from that dating situation because he knows you need to work on some other areas of your life before you start a romantic relationship. Maybe God has someone or something else in mind for you and even though this might "feel" right, he has another plan—after all, he is Creator of the universe.

See, if you believe that God is alive, that he is active in our lives, that his Spirit is moving, that God is almighty and sovereign, that he loves you and desires to build into you the character and attributes of Jesus Christ—then you have to believe that if it's in his plan, he'll make sure it gets done. On the other hand, if it's not in your life, God must have another plan for you.

Honestly, do you really think God is in Heaven thinking, "I'd really like Jim to go to that party, date that girl, go to that movie—but his parents keep messing it up! I guess I can't use Jim"? I don't think so. You have to believe that God is using all things, including your parents, to build things into your life. Proverbs 3:5, 6 includes a great promise:

> *"Trust in the LORD with all your heart; do not depend on your own understanding. Seek his will in all you do, and he will direct your paths" (NLT).*

There are going to be times when you just don't get what in

the world your parents are doing. There are going to be times when what they say or do doesn't make any sense. There are going to be times when what they say and do makes you confused, frustrated and even angry. In those times, you are going to have to hang on, trust God and look for what he might be teaching you and where he might be directing you.

I believe that when we pray, God always gives us an answer. That answer might be "Yes." That answer might be "No." That answer might be "Not now." Could it be that God is telling you "no" through your parents? Could he be telling you, "Not right now!"?

Have you ever had to baby-sit a little kid? You want to make a baby mad? Tell him "no" or "wait, not right now." Babies hate that. They cry, scream, stomp and whine. It's called "immaturity." That's what babies do. Do you disagree with your parents? That's going to happen . . . but don't be a baby. Maybe something else is going on. Maybe God is trying to tell you something.

3. What if the shoe were on the other foot?

If you were the parent, would you let your daughter date anyone she wanted? If you were the parent, would you let your son stay out as late as he wanted? If you were the parent, would you keep your nose out of your child's business? Knowing what you know about youth culture, if you were the parent, would you let your child attend unchaperoned parties? If you were the parent, would you let your child ride in a car with a 16-year-old driver?

I bet that most of you reading this book are answering "no." Why? Because you know the stuff that goes on "out there" in your schools, at your parties and in your cars. The truth is, you probably want your parents to allow you to do things that you would never allow your own children to do.

One of my biggest fears for my daughter Alison's dating life is that there are guys out there like me. I'm not stupid. I know what guys are like. I am one. When I was in high school, I was a Christian and I loved Jesus, but I also didn't have very good judgment. Now, as a dad, the shoe is on the other foot for me. There is a part of me that wants to build a fence around the house and fill the yard with land mines with a big sign that says, "Hey, all you creepy, perverted, hormone-infested, sex fiends: Stay away from my daughter!" Before you blow up at your parents over the call they've just made, stop and ask yourself, "What would I do if I were in their shoes?"

4. Obey in the Lord.

We've already said this, but I want to stress it again. If your parents make a decision, you must have the attitude that whatever they say, you'll obey. If you're a Christian, disobeying your parents is *not* an option. It is never God's will for you to disobey your parents (unless it is a sinful situation). There are no exceptions to this commandment from God. You will never read the words, "be true to yourself" or "follow your heart" in the Bible. On the contrary, you will read that the heart (your emotions) is a great deceiver. Jeremiah 17:9 says:

> *"The heart is deceitful above all things and beyond cure. Who can understand it?"*

There are going to be times when you will *feel* like the best thing to do is to disobey your parents. It will *make sense* to you that disobedience is justified. You will *think* that you know best and that your parents are wrong. Guess what? You might be right. They might have jumped to an incorrect assumption about your friends or activities. They might be dead wrong in their thinking and reasoning about the situation. If you were to poll your friends, most of them would probably agree with you that your parents are being too hard on you. But guess what else? God still commands you to obey your parents. He will never excuse disobedience because your parents are unreasonable, not understanding or unsympathetic. His Word is clear in Ephesians 6:1-3. According to verse three, the promise is that when you obey your parents, the quality of your life is going to be better.

What is God's goal for your life? (We've said this now about fifty times.) That's right. Maturity. God wants to build into you all of the mature character of his Son, Jesus. That includes love, joy, peace, patience, kindness, goodness, faithfulness, gentleness and self-control. He uses all kinds of things to accomplish that goal. There seems to be some confusion among Christians today. We believe that God's foremost goal for our lives is for us to be happy. We may think something like this: "If God loves me, I'll be happy all of the time, right?" Not necessarily. God's goal for us is to become more like his Son. Sometimes that means happiness. But sometimes it means suffering. Sometimes it means sacrificing what we desire for what God desires.

But God makes us a promise. He hasn't condemned us to a lifetime of misery under our parents' rule. He promises that when we live a life of obedience, it is all part of the abundant life that Jesus assured. God doesn't command obedience to hurt us. It's not like he is looking down on us from Heaven saying, "Hey, how can I mess up their social life today?" Remember, the only time God tells us "no" is when he has something better in store for us.

Getting Personal

1. *If you were a "real Christian," you wouldn't have disagreements with your parents, right? Why is this not necessarily true?*

2. *Why does anger present a dangerous opportunity to sin?*

3. *How is self-control evidence of maturity?*

4. *How can God be "telling you something" when you come up against a situation that you disagree with?*

5. *How can "putting the shoe on the other foot" help you better understand your parents' perspective?*

6. How can your heart deceive you into believing that disobedience is the right choice?

7. What is God's foremost goal for your life: to be happy or something else?

nine

Keep Talking

and Keep Trying

Chapter Nine

A couple of years ago, I had the opportunity to go to Kenya, Africa, on a short-term mission trip. Just before the conclusion of my trip, we visited a game preserve for a two-day safari. This was a dream come true for me. There I was, riding in a big Land Rover, trekking across the open plains of Africa. I looked out one window and saw a herd of zebra. A little further on . . . giraffe. But of course, the animal that we all wanted to see was a lion. We searched for hours. Massai tribesmen rode on the roof, trying to spot any signs of a lion. Finally, the Massai began pounding on the roof, pointing to some bushes and saying what sounded to me like, "Oobla, oobla, oobla."

There, lying in the shade, were three lions, stretched out, trying to stay cool. Around their mouths you could see dried blood from the previous night's kill. It was awesome. We pulled up in our truck no more than ten feet from where they were lying. Now, remember that I am an animal freak, so I wanted to get some great pictures. I was hanging out of the truck window, clicking away. One of the Massai whispered to me, "Oobla, oobla." I was thinking, "He really admires my new camera."

Well, I had a small problem. I couldn't get a good shot of the lion's face, so I did what any stupid American would do that had never been ten feet from a lion in an open field—I started meowing like a cat. (Give me a break, it seemed like a good idea at the time.) Let me give you some free advice. If you are ever in an open field, ten feet from a lion, don't meow like a cat. The head of one of the lions popped up, looked at me and snarled. Her back legs gathered under her and she prepared to jump. Meanwhile, I had stopped breathing and the Massai were now pounding the roof and screaming, "OOBLA, OOBLA, OOBLA." We had a small communication problem. See, "oobla" doesn't mean, "act like an idiot." It means, "shut up or she'll eat you."

One of the major problems today between teenagers and their parents is exactly this—communication. It's as if they speak different languages.

- How was school today? *Fine.*
- What did you do? *Nothing.*
- Who was there? *People.*
- How are you? *Fine.*
- Are you OK? *Yeah.*
- What's the matter? *Nothing.*
- What are you doing? *Nothing.*
- Did you hear me? *Whatever.*

Sound familiar? When was the last time you had a conversation with one of your parents that didn't involve your asking for something or arguing over some disagreement or problem?

It's very interesting to listen to the typical (non-) conversation that exists in an average family. It usually consists of one of the parents asking fifty questions and the teenager responding with grunts, groans, sighs and one-word answers—punctuated by rolling the eyes.

Think about it. When was the last time, if ever, that you remember sitting down with one of your parents (with no TV, no music and no time limit) and actually talking about stuff that was going on in your life? When was the last time, if ever, that you had a choice to make, and you asked your parents' opinion of your decision? This might be an overstatement, but most of the time we talk to our parents only when we need something. Things like, "Hey, Mom, can I have some money? Hey, Dad, can I borrow the car? Hey, can you bail me out of jail?"

Why is it that around the junior-high years, students often shut out their parents? It's like, all at once, their parents become the most ignorant people on the face of the earth. We would probably never say that out loud, but that's the way we often treat them. Why is that? I have a couple of thoughts.

1. They know us.

Often, the reason we avoid talking to parents or asking their opinions on a particular subject is that we realize that they know us pretty well. They may give us an answer we don't want to hear. One of the benefits of talking on the Internet is that you can be and say anything you want to be or say—and no one knows if it's true or not. Think about it. You can get on there and say that you are a rich, talented, beautiful super-model or an all-American athlete—and no one knows if you are bluffing or not. It's easy to hold a conversation when there is no accountability.

On the other hand, it's tough to sit and ask a hard question of someone who knows the real you, who knows your history, who knows your personality, who has spent years seeing you in action. I hear students say all the time, "I like to talk to my friends—they understand me." Maybe the bigger problem with your parents is that they understand you *too* well.

2. We're afraid of the truth.

Listen to this:

> *"For a time is coming when people will no longer listen to right teaching. They will follow their own desires and will look for teachers who will tell them whatever they want to hear. They will reject the truth and follow strange myths"* (2 Timothy 4:3, 4, NLT).

In these verses, Paul wrote to a young preacher named Timothy about the tendency of people to turn away from what they knew to be truth. To make themselves feel better, they would surround themselves with people who would say only things that they'd agree with. Don't we do the same thing? How many times have you felt strongly about something? What was the first thing you did? You probably found others who felt the same way about it. The last thing you wanted to do was to sit down and talk to someone else who felt differently.

Many times, I think we do that with our parents. We might say, "Oh, I know what they'll say before they say it. They'll say 'no,' they'll say 'you're not ready,' they'll say 'you're wrong.'" Even if we know deep down inside that they are probably right, we don't want to hear it.

So, what is the solution to communication problems? Here it is: Keep trying. Profound, isn't it? I believe that Satan hates your family. First Peter 5:8 says so:

> *"Be self-controlled and alert. Your enemy the devil prowls around like a roaring lion looking for someone to devour."*

Satan wants to destroy your family. Sometimes he does it by an all-out attack. But, more often than not, he chips away at it little bits at a time. If he can get you to stop communicating, it is only a matter of time until you and your parents are speaking "different languages." What can you do to break down the communication gap between your parents and yourself?

3. Do your part.

When I went to visit the Massai people of Kenya, how successful would my mission trip have been if I had gone with the attitude, "Hey, I speak the right language—if they don't understand me, it's their problem"? Obviously, the trip would have been a disaster. All too often, I think that's how teenagers approach their parents. Each speaks their own language and feels like the other doesn't understand them. What's the point of trying? The point is that if someone doesn't make the attempt, the relationship is doomed to failure. Listen to these words from Hebrews 12:14:

> *"Make every effort to live in peace with all men and to be holy; without holiness no one will see the Lord."*

The writer of Hebrews is saying that it is our responsibility as Christians to make the effort to cultivate right relationships with those around us. God has commissioned us to work hard, to do our best to do the right thing. Secondly, he uses the phrase, "every effort." When God says *every*, he means that he wants us to give it our all. He wants us to do everything within our power, including throwing out all limitations, and pursue the right thing.

I've heard people tell me that relationships are 50/50. That means that I need to give a little and you need to give a little and we meet somewhere in the middle. That means that neither one of us really gets what we want, but it's better than nothing. I don't like that definition. I think there has to be something better than that. I've also been told that relationships are 100/100. You give 100% and so will I, and we'll both be happy because we're both giving it our all. This sounds even better. I mean, who can argue that a relationship won't be great if both people are really trying? But there's a problem with this ratio as well. It's conditional. What if one person fails to deliver his 100% effort? Does that mean that the deal is off?

Some teenagers approach their parents like this. They say, "I'd talk to my parents *if* they would really listen. I'd honor my dad *if* he would start acting honorably. I'd obey my mom *if* she were more reasonable." When you sign on with God, you throw out all deals and buy into what is called "agapé love." *Agapé* (pronounced uh-gop-ay) is a Greek word that refers to unconditional love. There is no "if" in agapé love. This kind of affection loves in spite of, regardless of the circumstances, regardless of the outcome or the response of the recipient of that love.

There may be tons of things that your parents need to change or do differently, but you know what? You have no control over that. Remember, God is much more concerned with your actions and responses to the world that you live in. (You may have to trust that he is also working in your parents' lives . . . even if you can't see it right now.)

What if you approached your parents with the ratio of 100/0? You might say, "I will pour 100% of myself into this relationship and expect nothing in return. I will do my best to pursue peace with my parents, not because I might get something out of it, not because I want something, not so that they will do anything in return, but simply because I know this is what God wants me to do." You might say, "I will give 100% effort (that means hard work) in honoring my parents, not because they are the most honorable people in the world, but because I know that God has told me to do so." You might say, "I will do my best to open up communication with my parents and make 'every effort' to live at peace with them." Where do you start? How do you begin communicating with your parents?

One of my favorite movies is *What About Bob?*, a film about a neurotic, paranoid, psychiatric patient who is afraid of everything. One day, his psychiatrist counseled him to begin taking "baby steps." By this, he meant that in order to make progress towards healing, he would need to begin with a few little things each day. It's the same with communicating with your parents. It would be ridiculous to suggest that you have a two-hour in-depth conversation with your dad when the two of you haven't really spoken in months. It starts with "baby steps." Here are a few suggestions to get you started:

• *Cards and notes*
Write a simple note and leave it where your mom will find it. Say something like, "Mom, thanks for all you do around here. I don't say that enough. Love ya." Hide a note in your dad's car, in his golf clubs, wherever it might surprise him. Say something like, "Dad, I miss you when you're gone. Just wanted to say that I love you." Send an e-mail to them. (Remember that the goal is not to get them to do something—you're doing your 100% because it's what God wants you to do.)

• *Conversations*
It is so easy to respond to questions with grunts and one-word answers. What if you made a decision that you would use complete sentences? I know it sounds tough, but I believe if you tried, you could do it. If your mom asks how school was, don't say, "fine" or "bad." Use several words . . . in a row. "It was pretty good. I had a test in Algebra and I think I did pretty well on it." Try it—your mom will probably be left speechless. If you really want to freak out your parents (again, not the goal), try asking them about something in their life. "Dad, how was your day? Mom, what do you think I should do about so and so?" (Warning: Be ready to dial 911.)

• *Time*

Let me give you a clue. There will never be enough time to do everything. There will never be some open time where you will say, "Hey, I have nothing else to do. I think I'll go work on my relationship with Dad." Not going to happen. But what is true is that you always have time for the things that you consider a high priority. You usually have time to eat. You have time almost every day to hang out with friends, talk to them on the computer or on the phone, listen to music, watch TV and do homework. Why? Because these are things that you have decided have value (assuming you do your homework).

It's the same way with your parents. Make a decision that every day, you will spend some amount of time talking to your parents. Here's something that will freak you out. I heard a statistic one time that said that the average teenager spends around 18 seconds a day in conversation with his or her parents. 18 *seconds!* You know what that is? It's the natural result of speaking different languages—and it doesn't turn around just by accident. It has to be given value.

One day while we were in Africa, we took a four-hour hike up into the mountains to research some possible sites for our team to come and work on. One of the dangers of traveling in a foreign country is that sometimes (most times) the food can really mess up your digestive system (that's a nice way of saying, "you get diarrhea"). Anyway, about 30 minutes into our hike, one of our team, Darren, turned pale and had "the look." We had to complete our hike so we had one of our Massai guides take Darren back to the truck to rest.

Darren didn't speak Massai and the Massai didn't speak English but they managed as best they could. After awhile, Darren knew that nature was calling . . . fairly urgently. Through hand gestures and motions (that I don't want to think about), Darren was able to communicate his "need." The Massai took him to the edge of the village and pointed to the forest. A few yards outside the village, Darren found a small hut that would allow someone to fit inside, if that person squatted down. There was nothing else around so he assumed it was a Massai outhouse. Darren completed his "task" and returned to the truck to wait for us.

Later, on the ride back to the mission, Darren informed us of his small victory and the quaint little outhouse he had discovered. The Land Rover screeched to a halt and the missionary cried out, "Oh no!" Apparently, the quaint little "outhouse" wasn't really an outhouse at all. It was a special shelter for the chief to sit in during the day to get out of the hot sun. Darren had pretty much defiled the most sacred spot in the village. You know what Darren needed? A translator. A translator's job is to take two parties that can't communicate very well and bridge the gap between them.

I think we need the same thing. And you know what? We have one. He is the Holy Spirit. Jesus promised in John 14:26:
"But the Counselor, the Holy Spirit, whom the Father will send in my name, will teach you all things and will remind you of everything I have said to you."

God is not the kind of God who sits in Heaven and shouts down commands from on high. "Hey, you down there—good luck, hope you can do it." No, he promises to go through it with us. God doesn't just command us to work hard at peace, honor and obedience, or even take "baby steps" on our own, in our own strength. No, he promises to supply everything we need. Through Paul he assures us:
"I can do everything through him who gives me strength. . . . And my God will meet all your needs according to his glorious riches in Christ Jesus" *(Philippians 4:13, 19).*

God never commands us to do something and then leaves us hanging. He will do it with us. You know why? Because he loves us 100/0. He loves us unconditionally. He loves us the way that he wants us to love each other . . . including our parents. Is it easy? No. Is it a big deal? Yes. Is it worth it? Absolutely. No more excuses. It's time to communicate.

Getting Personal

1. *Would you say that you and your parents do or do not have a communication problem? Why?*

2. *When was the last time you and your parents had a conversation that didn't involve your asking for anything or your being in trouble?*

3. *Why do you sometimes avoid the truth?*

4. *Why would Satan want to destroy your family? How does breaking down communication help him to do this?*

5. *Why is 100/0 a better ratio than 100/100 or 50/50?*

6. What is the risk of the 100/0 ratio?

7. What are some "baby steps" you could take to get started?

8. Why is God more concerned with your "baby steps" than your parents' response?

9. How does the Holy Spirit work as a translator between you and your parents?

ten

10

Under Attack

Chapter Ten

One Friday night this past year I walked in the house and my wife Robin told me that a young man from the youth group, Justin, had called for me. Robin was concerned because he had quite a bit of panic in his voice. A few minutes later, the phone rang again. I answered it to hear a distraught, 16-year-old Justin fighting back tears and asking if we could talk. "What's going on, Justin?" I asked. "Give me a clue."
"I've had it. I want to divorce my dad," he responded.

Within the hour, Justin and his brother arrived and the story unfolded. Justin's parents had divorced several years earlier. Since then, Justin's mom had remarried and Justin had a tremendous relationship with his stepfather. I'm not going to pull any punches here—Justin's biological father was a real jerk. I hope that's not disrespectful, and I know that God loves him, but he acted in some very "jerky" ways. He was one of those guys who was very self-centered, who worked a lot, who missed most of Justin's life. Then, because he felt guilty about it, he rushed in and tried to make up for it all in one day. I knew a little about his reputation and Justin's story confirmed what I had heard.

This was Justin's weekend to live at his dad's house. The difficulty started when Justin had a school conflict with his dad's dinner plans. His dad said, "You never call me and tell me what's going on in your life." Justin reacted, "Maybe it's because you're not in my life and that's fine with me." Things got ugly fast. Yelling. Screaming. Tears. Slamming doors. "Call Jim."

I remember Justin saying, "I just wish I could divorce my dad." That scared me. Here's why. Justin was falling into a destructive pattern, a pattern that says, "When things get tough . . . leave." That's what happened with his parents. I don't know why his parents got a divorce and it's not my business to speculate on it. I do know that Justin caught the message, "When things get tough—quit, leave, divorce." So, let's say that Justin did divorce his father, which is legally possible in many states. What is going to happen when, later in life, his marriage hits some tough times? He's going to do what he's been trained to do—leave. What is he going to do with his own children when there is a big problem or conflict? Sure. He's going to quit, check out, walk away. That's the "normal" thing to do.

What I tried to communicate to Justin that night, and what I've tried to communicate to you in this book is that there is something bigger going on in your life than the "stuff" that you see and feel around you. God has a big plan for your life and he will use everything that is happening in your life now to prepare you for the next thing he has for you. How you deal with life situations now is training you for how you will respond to bigger and tougher situations later. If you are a quitter now, there's a pretty good chance you'll be a quitter later. But, if you are faithful in things now, you will probably be faithful in things later.

I believe that it is God's will that families stay together. I believe that divorce is way out of God's perfect plan. He says it right in Malachi 2:16:

> *"'I hate divorce,' says the LORD God of Israel. . . ."*

I believe that God wants Justin's father to be more involved in Justin's life, to be more supportive, to be a good and loving father. I believe that all of those things are consistent with what the Bible instructs parents to be. But all of that is between God and Justin's father. For Justin, God is much more concerned with his faithfulness in this tough situation. In our conversation that night, we discussed what he was going to do in the face of a bad situation. That included apologizing for speaking disrespectfully. It included disciplining himself to call his dad regularly to inform him about what was going on in his life. These were the right things for Justin to do. God was using this situation to build something bigger in his life.

Earlier, I made a statement that I believe Satan targets and schemes against people in order to achieve their downfall. The apostle Paul encourages us to be on our guard and be alert. He says in 2 Corinthians 2:11:

"So that Satan will not outsmart us. For we are very familiar with his evil schemes" (NLT).

You probably are very familiar with his evil schemes. One area he has singled out in his onslaught on teenagers pertains to love and sex. If Satan can get you to buy into his lie and trip you up in this area of your life, he knows that there is an extremely good chance he can get you to fall completely.

The other area that he attacks, sometimes in a more subtle way, is the family. If Satan can get you to have a warped view of what a relationship with a father should be like, then he can mess up your view of what a relationship with your Heavenly Father could be as well. If Satan can set a standard of disrespect, dishonor and disobedience in your response to authority in your life now, then later, when God commands you to follow him, go here, do this, say that, be holy, stay pure, obey his commandments—your natural response will be, "Sorry, won't do that." If Satan can set a pattern in your life that when things get tough you quit, then he can expect you to give up on God when the tough times come for you as a Christian.

Try sitting down with a girl who has been abused by her father and telling her that God is a loving father. She's had her fill of "loving fathers." Try explaining to a high-school guy whose father has walked out on him and his mother that

"Father God" loves him and is always available to him. You can expect the response, "Yeah, right, I've heard that before." If Satan can tear down the family, which is in many ways a "picture" of what God wants with us, he has come one step closer to destroying our relationship with God.

Last year I was involved in a Bible study where we each took turns sharing about some of the things God had brought us through in our lives. One dear friend of mine opened up her life and gave us a glimpse into what God had done for her. She came from a pretty rough family. No hugs. No pats on the back. No affection. No encouragement. In four years of playing varsity sports, her parents didn't come to even one of her games. In one heated argument, her mom blurted out, "I don't know why I had you. I should have just aborted you."

Wow! Can you imagine being told that by the one person on earth who should have been the most encouraging, the most loving, the most supportive? My friend was devastated. Through much of her life, she struggled with a need for affection, depression and poor self-image. The only thing that rescued her from a life of insecurity and low self-esteem was the realization that God valued her. In his Word, in prayer and in worship, she discovered that she mattered because she mattered to God. What Satan had meant for her defeat, God used to bring her closer than she ever thought possible.

A few years ago, a boy in our ministry was killed in a tragic car accident. While going through some of his possessions, one of his close friends found a letter he had written a few days before his death. She read the letter at his funeral. It contained his thoughts and discoveries about life from his short years. One phrase stood out that he had written to his friend. It simply said, "Keep an eternal perspective." What he meant was this: It's not all about the here and now. Everything that we face now is part of a broader plan that God has for our lives. There's something bigger going on. That's great wisdom from a 17-year-old. And that's the message I want to leave with you. Keep an eternal perspective.

God, your "heavenly parent," wants you to have a healthy, vibrant, loving and communicating relationship with your earthly parents. He knows that when you do that, it will contribute to your relationship with him. And of all of the things you can say about Satan, you can't accuse him of being stupid. He knows that if he can undermine your relationship with your mom and dad, he has his foot in the door to subvert your relationship with God as well. But, if you are aware of his evil schemes to take you down, you can overcome him by the power of God in your life.

Getting Personal

1. In Justin's story, what was the danger of "divorcing" his dad?

2. What are some things that Justin could do to improve his relationship with his father?

3. How does Satan's attack on your family have the potential to harm your relationship with God as well? Are there specific instances when he has accomplished that in your life?

4. Why does God "hate divorce"?

5. What does it mean to "keep an eternal perspective"?

6. How should keeping an eternal perspective help you to deal with the tough things in life?

eleven

Final Thoughts

Chapter Eleven

Well, I hope I haven't just thrown a bunch of advice at you. I've tried to take some biblical wisdom and show you that God has an awesome plan for your life. He loves you so much and wants nothing less than to build into you all of the character, integrity and attributes of his Son, Jesus. He cares about your relationship with your parents. In today's world, biological or adoptive parents, stepparents, foster parents, grandparents or guardians might fill that parental role. God wants to use whoever fills that role in your life to accomplish eternal results in you. If God has taught you something about his will for your life in the pages of this book and it has caused you to make a decision concerning something in your life that needs to change, let me both encourage and warn you.

1. Get started now!

Now means "now." It doesn't mean "someday." It doesn't mean, "right after I do this one thing." It means "from this point on." God never indicated or even hinted that following him would be easy, simple or convenient. As a matter of fact, most of what he will call you to do is pretty "countercultural." (That's a big word that means God is telling you to be different and go against the flow.) Stop making excuses and throw out the "what if's" and do what he is telling you to do (and you know what that is for you).

2. Be warned!

I used to think that Satan's goal for our lives was to do big horrible things. You know, like things you hear on the news: school shootings, war, rape, murder, cutting up people with chain saws . . . gross stuff like that. But you know what I tend to think now? Yeah, sometimes, Satan works in those kinds of ways. But what he really wants you to do is . . . nothing. Yep, nothing. See, if he can keep you doing nothing, then you are no threat. But the moment that you make a decision to move off-center and actually follow God, then he gets worried—and when he gets worried, he usually attacks.

Have you ever been on a retreat or to a week of camp or some super-spiritual mountaintop experience? I mean, you feel closer to God than you ever have before. But then, have you noticed that when you get home, things seem worse than ever before? Your mom turns into the wicked witch of the north, your dad becomes a dictator, your dog stinks more than usual, you're convinced that your little brother may possibly be the antichrist. Why is that? I think it's because Satan gets worried and throws extra forces at you. It's like he says, "Oh no you don't, get back there in line and do nothing . . . stay the same." Be warned, if you take this parent stuff seriously, Satan is going to get worried. It will probably get harder before it gets easier.

3. The only way to follow God on the outside is to have him on the inside.

Almost everything in this book, or in the Bible for that matter, is impossible for you to pull off on your own. How many times have you made a New Year's resolution or made a promise that you were going to do something? You said, "I really mean it this time." Yeah, me too. Thousands of times. We mean well, and we really want to do it! But over time, the commitment starts to fade, other things get in the way, conflicts arise, no one is there to encourage us. Pretty soon, it's back to business as usual. The *only* solution is for us to spend time with God every day—in his Word, on our knees, praying for our parents, our families, our willpower and our faithfulness. It's the only way. If we try another path, we will fail.

You know, most times, when you come to the end of a book, you slam it closed, check it off as "mission accomplished" and move on to the next thing. Before you close this book, I want you to do something. Pray. I know, you pray all of the time. This time, I want you to pray for your parents. Pray that God will bless them and move in them and they will grow to be the godly people that he wants them to be. That might mean praying that one day they will come to know him as Lord and Savior. Don't pray that they will do something for you or change something in your favor. Just pray for them.

Secondly, pray a prayer of confession and repentance. Be honest with God; admit to him the areas where you need to grow, change, honor and obey. Don't make excuses or offer him reasons why you make mistakes. Don't tell him it would be easier *if* he would change a few things down here. Just honestly humble yourself before him and tell him where you've blown it.

Finally, ask him to build you into the godly young man or woman he wants you to be. Get this. Give him "permission" to do *anything* in your life he deems necessary to accomplish this goal. Wow! Scary prayer. See, it's easy to pray, "Bless the poor people in Africa." It's easy to pray, "Help me to be a good Christian." It's a whole lot tougher to say, "God, do whatever it takes to get me to the place that you want me to be." That takes guts. That takes faith. Go ahead, right now; spend some time in prayer. Then, we'll finish up.

Remember that little deer in chapter one? It was all about getting on the truck and going to the place that the little deer was meant to be. And the sooner the deer cooperated, the sooner the mission could have been accomplished. God has been patiently waiting on you for this moment in time. The moment in time when you say to him, "Here am I, your will be done." When a person prays that prayer, things start to happen. God loves you and he has an awesome plan for your life and for your family. He's been ready and waiting on you. NOW it's time to get started. May God bless you and your family.

Getting Personal

1. *What new things has God revealed about your parents and you?*

2. *Why does Satan attack those who have made a decision to begin following God's plan for their lives?*

3. *What does this statement mean: "The only way to follow God on the outside is to have him on the inside"?*

4. *How does one come to have God on the inside?*

5. *What has God been teaching you about what he wants to do in your relationship with your parents?*

6. *What is standing in the way of that becoming a reality?*

7. *What are you going to do now?*

Excerpt from *What's the Big Deal? about sex*
Chapter Three

God created man but it wasn't good for him to be alone. So, God created woman to be man's partner, to help and complement him.

We talked about the differences between these two creations. Men and women are different:
1. physically, in their "plumbing" and a whole lot more
2. emotionally, in the man's need to feel adequate versus the woman's need to feel loved
3. mentally, in their thinking processes and chemical make-up of the brain
4. relationally, in which men are to be the initiators and women are to be the responders

We started with a simple question: "Do you see yourself dating, falling in love, marrying and being involved in a sexual relationship?"

The next question is, "If you do, what *kind* of a relationship do you want?" If you agree with what Hollywood, rock stars and pop culture define as love, good luck. However, very few of us want that kind of love. We want something far better.

Recently, I had the privilege of participating in an open forum, a debate where I presented my views and a woman who had a Ph.D. in Sexual Deviancy and Marriage and Family argued the opposite position. (How would you explain to your mom that you were majoring in sexual deviancy?) The assigned question we were to address was, "Are we failing our youth in terms of sex education?"

The doctor presented her viewpoint first. Her answer could be summed up as: "Yes, we are failing our children. We need more education and more accessible contraceptives (condoms, pills and abortion). Teenagers are going to have sex. It's unrealistic to expect anything less. There is no way to stop them. We need to prevent pregnancy and keep sex 'safe.'"

This argument always puzzles me. Ask your medical doctor if he or she believes in "safe sex." Follow that question with, "If your own son or daughter were going to have sex with someone you knew was HIV positive, would the presence of a condom set your mind at ease?" Watch the doctor stutter around with an answer.

My answer was, "No, we're not failing them. They are living up to society's expectations for them. We have told them, 'Hey, we give up. You have sexual urges. Fulfill them. OK, it would probably be better if you waited, but we know you won't. So here is a condom—protect yourself.'"

I think our government agrees more with the Ph.D.'s premise, having spent billions of dollars on contraceptives and "safe sex" programs as opposed to a few million dollars on abstinence programs. Why? Because that's what the news media, MTV and Hollywood say our kids want to hear and what they need. But is it, really?

In a recent poll, nearly 9 out of 10 high-school students questioned said they didn't want condoms handed out in their school or in the vicinity of their school. In another national poll, when questioned about the number one issue that needs to be addressed with teenagers, 99% responded, "How do I say no to sexual pressure?" They listed this issue above drugs, alcohol, violence, suicide, pregnancy and pornography.[1]

Sure, many kids are having sex. Some studies estimate that two-thirds to three-quarters of all graduating seniors have had at least one sexual encounter. A more recent survey suggests that fewer than 25% have actually "gone all the way." It depends on who you ask and who is being honest. However, almost all young people are saying, "We want to be able to say no; help us know how to say no. Give us a better reason to wait than to give in."

That's the biggest question that has to be answered: Why? Why wait for marriage? Why be monogamous (staying with one partner for life)? Why not have sex now? Let's look at some possible answers!

1. Because you might die!

Believe it or not, this is not a good enough answer. Fear is not an effective deterrent. Let's look at the facts: First of all, con-

doms fail one out of six times—not great odds. (Even the condom package states that a condom is no guarantee against disease.) The AIDS virus is so small, it is able to pass through the
microscopic holes in a latex condom. "Safe sex" or "smart sex"
is a joke! If you'll notice, the media now call it "*safer* sex."

Secondly, most guys don't wear a condom regularly.[2] Many
guys I have talked to have promised to "try to remember." If
two people are going at it hot and heavy, and someone says,
"Sorry, I didn't bring a condom," rarely will both agree to call
it quits. They're probably not going to just say, "Hey, let's go
bowling instead."

In the next few years, over 100 million people will be HIV positive or will have already died. Some estimate that at the present
time, one in 75 guys and one in 200 girls are already infected
and don't even know it. One new HIV infection occurs each 54
seconds; one death from AIDS occurs each 9 minutes; 267 new
AIDS cases are reported each day.[3]

AIDS has been the sixth leading cause of death among 15-24
year olds since 1991.[4] At the present time, if you contract AIDS,
you are as good as dead. There is no cure. Worse, you may not
even be aware that you are a carrier for 10 years or more. By
that time, most will be married, possibly with children; and, if
you are a carrier, all of your family members could be infected.

I recently met a man who had become a Christian 10 years
ago. Since giving his life to Christ, he had been completely

sexually abstinent. He is a talented songwriter and musician. We regularly sing worship choruses in our church that he has written. A few weeks ago, he was diagnosed with full-blown AIDS. His sexual activity before he became a Christian has caught up with him. God will always forgive sin, but the consequences of choices we made years ago may haunt us for the rest of our lives . . . and may even end them.

But you know what? Fear of death is not enough to force you to be abstinent.

2. OK, how about, because you might get pregnant?

Again, not a good enough reason. Every day 2,700 teens become pregnant. Every 24 hours, another 3,000 become sexually active and lose their virginity.[5] Some people might say, "It's OK, I'm on the pill." Sorry, not a good answer! The pill is not totally effective in older women, let alone with a teenage girl who hasn't established a regular menstrual cycle.

More than one million teenage girls become pregnant each year. Of that one million, just over three in ten choose to abort the baby. In 1994, that added up to 298,000 teen abortions for one year. As a country, the U.S. has topped 4,000 abortions a day. One-third of your generation has already been aborted.[6]

I don't think that anything you read here or see on TV or hear from a sermon will ever "scare" you into not having sex in the long term. Maybe it would work for a week or two. I could tell you a sad story of a life devastated by AIDS or show you a picture of an abortion and you would respond, "Gross!" and determine that that life wasn't for you. But your fear-inspired response would eventually fade. Why?

1. Because very few people (especially teenagers) think that they are going to die anytime soon.

2. Very few teenage girls think that they could really get pregnant. That happens to "other people." Nearly every teenage couple who has found themselves in this situation and come to me for help has always said the same thing: "We never thought this would happen to us."

The sexual drive is very strong. Faced with sexual temptation, you can rationalize away your fears and override common sense. I am convinced that no one can "scare" you into not having sex.

Well then, what's the answer? Why shouldn't you have sex before marriage? I believe that this is a big question and to answer it, we have to go to a higher level. Higher than Top 40 music, the newest MTV vj, blockbuster Hollywood movie or U.S. Surgeon General.

Let's ask God. He created sex. What does he think about it?

Notes

What's the Big Deal? About Sex

[1]"What the World's Teenagers Are Saying," *U.S. News & World Report* (June 30, 1986), p. 68.

[2]Henshaw, S., "Unintended Pregnancy in the United States," *Family Planning Perspectives* (1998), volume 30, pp. 24-29.

[3]Dorgan, C.A., *Statistical Record of Health & Medicine*, (NY: Gale Research, 1995), Table 48, pp. 315, 316.

[4]*HIV/AIDS Surveillance Report #7*, 1995, Atlanta, GA: U.S. Department of Health and Human Services, Centers for Disease Control.

[5]Henshaw, S., *U.S. Teenage Pregnancy Statistics*, (New York, NY: The Alan Guttmacher Institute, August 15, 1997).

[6]Henshaw, S., "Unintended Pregnancy in the United States," *Family Planning Perspectives* (1998), volume 30, pp. 24-29.

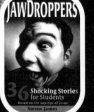